TRUSTEES OF THE MERCIFUL

AN INTRODUCTION TO BAHÁ'Í ADMINISTRATION

TRUSTEES OF THE MERCIFUL

AN INTRODUCTION TO BAHÁ'Í ADMINISTRATION

by

ADIB TAHERZADEH

Illustrated by
Lesley Taherzadeh O'Mara

GEORGE RONALD
OXFORD

George Ronald, Publisher
Oxford
www.grbooks.com

1st edition Bahá'í Publishing Trust, London, UK, 1972
2nd edition 2009 including author's revisions (1999) updated in 2008
This edition, George Ronald Publisher, 2015

A catalogue record for this book is available from the British Library

ISBN 978-0-85398-592-1

Cover design: Steiner Graphics

CONTENTS

FOREWORD

Trustees of the Merciful was first published in 1972 to coincide with the 50th year of the Formative Age of the Faith.

The first two chapters aim to emphasize the spirit that animates the Administrative Order of Bahá'u'lláh and to indicate the spiritual attitude that must characterize the members of the institutions of the Cause.

The third chapter surveys the unfoldment of the Administrative Order during the first 50 years of the Formative Age and outlines certain statistical information related to the expansion of the Faith during that period.

Without giving additional statistical details, this work is now updated to include further important developments that have taken place in the Bahá'í community since its first publication.

A fourth chapter has been added which, it is hoped, will further assist the reader in the study of the spiritual aspects of the Administrative Order of Bahá'u'lláh.

Adib Taherzadeh
Haifa, June 1999

INTRODUCTION

The passing of 'Abdu'l-Bahá in 1921 marks on the one hand the closing of the most glorious age of the Bahá'í Dispensation, the Heroic or Apostolic Age and, on the other, the opening of the Formative Age which is an age of transition and which must ultimately usher in the Golden Age of the Faith when the sovereignty of Bahá'u'lláh and the World Order of His Faith are fully established throughout this planet.

The Heroic Age, which began with the Declaration of the Báb in 1844 and the duration of which was 77 years, witnessed the appearance of two Manifestations of God, the Báb and Bahá'u'lláh, as well as the establishment of a mighty Covenant whose Centre was the person of 'Abdu'l-Bahá. In that age the Revelation of God shed its splendours for well nigh 50 years upon this world. The spiritual energies destined to revitalize the whole human race and establish in the fullness of time a new World Order, whose glory the Prophets of the past had foretold, were released to mankind.

The Martyr-Prophet of the Faith, the Primal Point 'from which have been generated all created things',[1] in the first period of that age sounded the trumpet call of the dawn of a new Day and at the end, through His martyrdom, shed an imperishable lustre upon the Cause of God.

In the second period of that age, Bahá'u'lláh, the Supreme Manifestation of God, at whose advent 'the hearts of the entire company' of God's 'Messengers and Prophets' were proved,[2] 'Whose presence' Moses 'hath longed to attain', for 'Whose love' Jesus 'ascended to heaven', 'the beauty of Whose countenance' Muḥammad 'had yearned to behold' and 'for Whose sake' the Báb 'offered up His life',[3] revealed Himself and, with the outpourings of His Revelation, 'breathed a new life into every human frame'.[4] It was in this period

– a period that lasted almost 40 years – that the teachings, the laws and ordinances of a Faith which is destined to regulate the life of the human race and govern the operation of its worldwide institutions for a period of no less than a thousand years were revealed and promulgated.

After the ascension of Bahá'u'lláh it was 'Abdu'l-Bahá, the 'Mystery of God',[5] 'He round Whom all names revolve',[6] who, during the 29 years constituting the third and final period of the Heroic Age, enriched and interpreted the holy writings; encompassed the Cause of God within His soul, preserved it from the onslaught of the breakers of the Covenant of Bahá'u'lláh, promoted its interests in the face of bitter opposition and propagated its message to the western world.

The passing of 'Abdu'l-Bahá marks the rise of the Administrative Order and ushers in the Formative Age. The central figure of this age is Shoghi Effendi, the Guardian of the Cause of God. He it is who was extolled by 'Abdu'l-Bahá as 'that primal branch of the Divine and sacred Lote-Tree', the 'priceless pearl' and 'the Light that . . . shineth from the Dayspring of Divine Guidance'.[7] For 36 years Shoghi Effendi guided the Bahá'í world in the building of the foundations of the Administrative Order, the features of which were clearly delineated by Bahá'u'lláh and 'Abdu'l-Bahá. He has left behind, in his voluminous writings and in his letters to individuals and Spiritual Assemblies, a great wealth of guidance which will direct, assist and inspire the Bahá'í world in the manifold tasks which confront it throughout the Formative Age.

The first 25 years of the Guardian's ministry constitute the first epoch of the Formative Age. The second epoch began in 1946, witnessed the passing of Shoghi Effendi in 1957 and ended in 1963 soon after the Universal House of Justice came into being. It announced in October 1963 the commencement of the third epoch, which lasted 23 years. In January 1986 the Bahá'í world was informed that the Formative Age had entered its fourth epoch.

The Universal House of Justice, this majestic institution which Bahá'u'lláh has ordained to be the supreme body of the Faith and upon which He has conferred infallible guidance, is today directing the Bahá'ís in the same task of raising the institutions of the Faith throughout the world.

In this Dispensation the most meritorious of all deeds has always been teaching the Cause of God. Yet in each period of the development of the Cause the believers have been faced with a specific task which demanded their complete and wholehearted attention. During the early days of the inception of the Faith, for example, the followers of the Báb often had to take up the sword and defend themselves against the fierce onslaughts launched by their enemies. In those days the call to action often sounded, as in Mullá Ḥusayn's immortal phrase 'Mount your steeds, O heroes of God!'[8]

In a later period, however, during Bahá'u'lláh's ministry, the believers were given a different task to perform: this time they were to put the sword away and teach the Cause with the utmost love and wisdom and even to give their lives willingly if the occasion demanded it. Many in that period drank the cup of martyrdom with joy and thankfulness and, with their lifeblood, proclaimed the Cause of God to multitudes.

During the ministry of 'Abdu'l-Bahá, although the believers continued to teach the Cause in the same way, the emphasis was changed. In this period the Covenant of God was violated, an act which brought in its wake a crisis of such magnitude that the protection of the Cause of God from the onslaught of the breakers of the Covenant took precedence over all other things. In this period the believers rallied around 'Abdu'l-Bahá, the Centre of the Covenant, and with determination and steadfastness protected the Cause of God from the attacks of the unfaithful.

In the Formative Age the main task given to the Bahá'ís, in addition to teaching and proclaiming the Cause and developing Bahá'í communities, is building the Administrative Order of Bahá'u'lláh. The believers work together for the establishment of Local and National Spiritual Assemblies in every part of the globe. The phenomenal increase in the number of these divine institutions and the need for their consolidation makes it necessary for Bahá'ís to deepen themselves in the verities of the Faith and the principles of the Administrative Order. Indeed, one of the major responsibilities placed on the shoulders of the members of the Spiritual Assemblies is that they should acquaint themselves fully with the administrative principles of the Faith delineated by Bahá'u'lláh, 'Abdu'l-Bahá and Shoghi Effendi.

Matters connected with the administration of the Faith or the form of the Administrative Order itself are not dealt with in the pages that follow. The aim is, rather, to trace the origin of the Administrative Order, to outline the spiritual standards and principles that govern the workings of the Spiritual Assembly, to emphasize the importance of understanding the spirit of the Administrative Order and of conforming to it and, finally, to describe the unfoldment of the administrative institutions of the Faith during the first 50 years of the Formative Age and beyond, up to the present time.

DIVINE REVELATION

The Word of God

One of the teachings which Bahá'u'lláh has unequivocally proclaimed is that the established religions of the world are divine in origin and that their Founders are the Manifestations of God who, through their appearance have, in every age, released into the world spiritual energies designed to uplift humanity and to further its progress.

The vehicle and carrier of these energies in every Dispensation has been the word of God revealed by His Manifestations. Their word has been creative and, by virtue of its potency and influence, has penetrated into the hearts of people thereby creating, in every age, a new civilization and a new race of men. The revelation of the words of God can be likened to the falling rain. At the time that it falls every plant is directly refreshed by its animating force. When it ceases to fall, however, the water of life can only be obtained at a reservoir created by the rainfall. Similarly, the word of God, revealed by each Manifestation, has given new life to those who came directly in touch with it. In every age the creative power of the word bestows everlasting life and the spirit of faith upon those disciples who are privileged to be in the presence of the Manifestation of God. But when the Prophet passes away and the vernal showers of revelation cease to pour, the faithful mass of the believers turn to the repository of the revealed word – the scriptures that have been left behind.

In past Dispensations the believers filled their vessels from this spiritual reservoir which contained the water of life. They first drank from it and then bestowed its life-giving waters upon others. In this analogy of the reservoir, however, if people were allowed to touch the water with their hands, to put their cups and vessels into it for the purpose of distributing it to others and to immerse themselves in its depths, then, over a period of time, the purity of the water was lost. Similarly, by having free access to the spiritual reservoir of the teachings and the words of God, by introducing into it unwholesome ideas, theories and interpretations and by mischievously manipulating the Faith of God, the followers adulterate the water of life and its purity is lost for ever.

The followers of each religion first received their inspiration from their scriptures and then imparted the healing message of their Prophet to others. In old Dispensations the believers were left free to interpret the word of God in accordance with their own understanding. People, therefore, introduced their own crude ideas into the Faith of God. Soon the purity of the teachings was lost, the followers were divided and schism was introduced into religion. For example, the body of Muḥammad was not yet buried when His followers were already divided into two major sects which soon produced numerous others. The pure, redeeming word of God fell into wicked hands and was manipulated for purely selfish reasons. This has been the pattern of past religions.

In this Dispensation, which is the consummation of past religions and cycles and which ushers in the advent of the 'Day of God',[9] the Revelation of Bahá'u'lláh has some unique features through which the unity of the community is safeguarded. One such is the authenticity and the immensity of the revealed word. Unlike Dispensations of the past, all the words of Bahá'u'lláh were written down by His amanuensis at the time of revelation. There is thus no shadow of doubt about their authenticity.

In contrast to what amounted to a few isolated showers in the older Dispensations, the word of God in this age poured down upon humanity in mighty torrents for a period of no less than 40 years, leaving behind the vast ocean of Bahá'í scriptures. So rapid has been the revelation of the word of God in this day that within the span of one hour the equivalent of a thousand verses were revealed by Bahá'u'lláh. He Himself, towards the end of His earthly life, testified that if all the revealed words were to be compiled it would produce almost a hundred volumes.

The Covenant of Bahá'u'lláh

A second distinguishing feature is a special gift of Bahá'u'lláh to mankind. This gift is the person of 'Abdu'l-Bahá. He it is who was created especially by God to act, after the passing of Bahá'u'lláh, as a mighty container and reservoir for the great ocean of His Revelation. For Bahá'u'lláh did not leave His word and His Revelation open to all after His ascension. Rather, He entrusted them to 'Abdu'l-Bahá. In His Will, written in His own hand, He appointed 'Abdu'l-Bahá as the Centre of His Covenant and enjoined upon all the believers to turn to Him in order to receive their portion of the bounties of God vouchsafed to mankind by His Revelation. To no one else did He give the right to interpret His writings, to add or to take away even a dot from whatever had been revealed. Only 'Abdu'l-Bahá could explain the meaning and purpose of the words of Bahá'u'lláh. Thus the mighty ocean of Revelation that was left behind by Bahá'u'lláh was placed within the person of 'Abdu'l-Bahá. In order to protect it from the hands of the unfaithful He acted as a wall around it and sealed it off from people's interference. So thoroughly did He embody and encompass the Revelation of Bahá'u'lláh within His soul that, after the ascension of Bahá'u'lláh, it was only through 'Abdu'l-Bahá that the redeeming power of His Faith and all the spiritual energies released by Him could flow to humanity.

Although not a Manifestation of God, 'Abdu'l-Bahá had, by virtue of being the container of the ocean of Bahá'u'lláh's Revelation, the authority of the Manifestation conferred on Him. Within His soul this great ocean surged for 29 years and He bestowed its life-giving waters upon thousands of men and women throughout the East and the West. During this period, however, many unscrupulous attempts were made from within the community to destroy the Cause of God and to break through the walls which protected that ocean, and many outstanding followers of the Faith rebelled against the Centre of the Covenant in order to promote their own selfish desires, to introduce their own ideas into the teachings, to divide the Faith of God and consequently to contaminate the water of life. But the Covenant of Bahá'u'lláh was based on a very firm foundation and the walls around the ocean were impregnable. Many heroic souls, devoted and faithful, served 'Abdu'l-Bahá with the utmost sincerity and faith; they rallied around Him and, like lions, defended the Covenant of Bahá'u'lláh against the onslaught of the unfaithful so that, at the end, they handed down to this generation, and generations yet unborn, the unadulterated word of God, the pure water of life, which in the fullness of time will revivify the souls of all humanity.

The Formative Age

With the passing of 'Abdu'l-Bahá in 1921, the Formative Age began. The springtime was ended and the early stages of the summer season

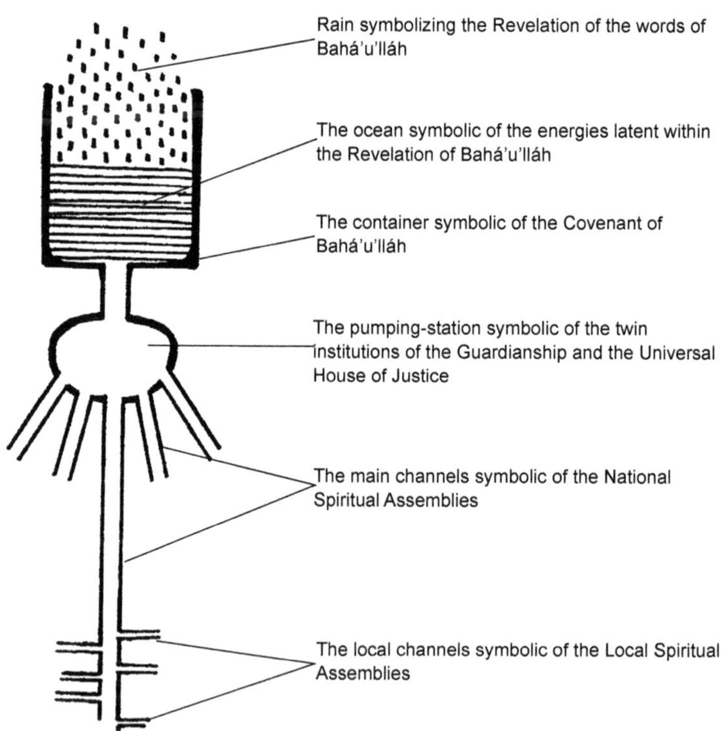

were ushered in. The great, the everlasting Covenant of God with humankind for this Dispensation, as distinct from the Covenant of Bahá'u'lláh with His followers, was now completed. All that God had bestowed upon humanity in this day may be said to consist of two things; one, the ocean of Bahá'u'lláh's Revelation (which also includes that of the Báb) and the other, its container, 'Abdu'l-Bahá. This was God's part of the Covenant.

The believers in the Formative Age had now to play their parts, as bidden by 'Abdu'l-Bahá in His Will and Testament, in the building up of institutions which were to act as channels designed to carry to every part of the planet the water of life which constituted the ocean of Bahá'u'lláh's Revelation. This is mankind's part in the great Covenant of God. Knowing their inadequacy and immaturity, 'Abdu'l-Bahá did not leave the believers alone in this task. He gave them Shoghi Effendi, whom He described as a pearl, unique and priceless, the 'primal branch of the Divine and sacred Lote-Tree', a light that 'shineth from the Dayspring of Divine Guidance',[10] the 'Sign of God on earth', the Guardian of the Cause of God and the Expounder and Interpreter of His Word. During the ministry of Shoghi Effendi the outpourings of Bahá'u'lláh's Revelation, pure and unadulterated, reached the believers through the institution of the Guardianship. The blueprint of the institutions, local, national and international – the channels designed to carry the water of life – had already been given by Bahá'u'lláh and 'Abdu'l-Bahá. Shoghi Effendi's task was that of the builder.

Following the analogy of the reservoir and the channels, it could be said that Shoghi Effendi acted as a pumping station connecting the ocean of Bahá'u'lláh's Revelation to a vast network of Local and National Assemblies. As the water supply is pumped out from the reservoir, first into the main channels and then into local pipes from which, pure and uncontaminated, it runs into every home, similarly, the world-vitalizing forces of the Faith of Bahá'u'lláh poured out from its World Centre through the Guardian into the National Assemblies and through these to the Local Assemblies all over the world. In this way the spirit of the Faith flowed to people without being adulterated by human beings. With the establishment of the Universal House of Justice, some time after the passing of Shoghi Effendi, the crowning edifice of the Administrative Order of Bahá'u'lláh was erected. Today the world-vivifying forces of the Faith, contained within the ocean of Bahá'u'lláh's Revelation, stream out from the Universal House of Justice into a vast network of National and Local Spiritual Assemblies bestowing spiritual life upon multitudes in every part of the world.

The outpouring of these forces is not limited to the Spiritual Assemblies. There is another channel through which these same forces flow to invigorate the Bahá'í community as well as the National and Local Spiritual Assemblies. This channel, usually referred to as the appointed arm of the Administrative Order, constitutes the institution of the Hands of the Cause and the Continental Boards of Counsellors with their Auxiliary Board members and assistants. A brief reference will be made in the following pages to this institution and to the vital role it plays in the growth and development of the Bahá'í community.

THE DIVINE INSTITUTIONS

Functioning of Spiritual Assemblies

The Spiritual Assemblies are divine institutions created by Bahá'u-'lláh. Upon those who serve on them He has bestowed an inestimable bounty, enabling them to take part in the erection of the framework of His World Order, now in its embryonic form. Great as this privilege is, members of these institutions are faced with staggering responsibilities for they can either, by means of applying the spiritual principles enshrined in the Administrative Order, establish strong and healthy Assemblies, firmly grounded and harmoniously functioning, or alternatively, degenerate into a mere body without spirit, well organized yet full of tension, problems, frictions and misunderstandings.

The Bahá'ís in the early days, those who lived and laboured in the Heroic Age, did not have these responsibilities or problems. Having come in direct contact with the Supreme Manifestation of God and the Centre of His Covenant, they had become a new creation endowed with divine qualities, utterly oblivious of themselves and wholly attracted to Bahá'u'lláh. Intoxicated by the wine of His utterances and completely devoted to Him, these holy souls, like plants in the spring season, were refreshed by the vernal showers of His Revelation. They drew their strength and sustenance directly and independently from the Centre of the Cause. These early believers had direct communication with Bahá'u'lláh and 'Abdu'l-Bahá and a great many of the Tablets we have today were revealed in answer to their questions. In that age there were no grounds for ill-feeling or misunderstanding, tension or friction among the believers, for they had no community life; it was then that the Cause produced its spiritual giants.

However, in the Formative Age the followers of Bahá'u'lláh must work together in Bahá'í communities. The vernal showers of

Bahá'u'lláh's Revelation have ceased and the spirit of the Cause of God, that water of life which animated a band of God-intoxicated heroes in an earlier age, can today reach and refresh the believers only through the institutions of a divinely-ordained Order. The Guardian, who laid the foundations of this Order and whose spirit will undoubtedly dominate the entire period of the Formative Age of the Faith, in speaking of the birth of the Administrative Order has summarized this process in these words:

> The moment had now arrived for that undying, that world-vitalizing Spirit that was born in Shíráz, that had been rekindled in Ṭihrán, that had been fanned into flame in Baghdád and Adrianople, that had been carried to the West, and was now illuminating the fringes of five continents, to incarnate itself in institutions designed to canalize its outspreading energies and stimulate its growth.[11]

This world-vitalizing spirit was released to the believers by the persons of Bahá'u'lláh and 'Abdu'l-Bahá during the Heroic Age of the Faith but Shoghi Effendi has, in the above passage, made it clear that this same spirit which quickens the souls and bestows the gift of faith is now, in the Formative Age, flowing through the institutions of the Faith, the Spiritual Assemblies which will, in the future, evolve into Local and National Houses of Justice. It follows therefore that a Local Spiritual Assembly becomes the means through which the forces of the Revelation of Bahá'u'lláh can reach a locality, enabling the believers to proffer its life-giving energies to their fellow-citizens. It is important to realize that what confirms the faith of the individual in Bahá'u'lláh is the spiritual forces latent within His Revelation, and since these forces flow through the institutions of His Faith, the Spiritual Assembly, acting as a channel, assumes a vital role in releasing the spiritual energies emanating from the ocean of the Revelation of Bahá'u'lláh within the city, town or village.

When there are not enough believers to form a Local Spiritual Assembly, a Bahá'í group, which consists of two to eight believers, provides this channel, for the group may be considered to be the embryo of an Assembly. An isolated believer, who acts as a nucleus of an Assembly, can also become a channel through whom the world-vitalizing spirit of the Faith will flow to others.

All this indicates that the local, national and international institutions of the Faith, being the carriers of the spirit of Bahá'u'lláh's Revelation, are indispensable means for the propagation of the Cause of Bahá'u'lláh throughout the world.

The Spiritual Assembly is not merely a meeting of nine believers; it is rather a divine institution in which the members become instrumental for the flow of the spirit. Members of the Spiritual Assemblies often come from backgrounds which are socially, intellectually and spiritually different. Young and old, rich and poor, literate and illiterate, veteran and newly enrolled, all may sit together as members of a Spiritual Assembly. This diversity of thought, of culture, of customs and background, which could give rise to such incompatibility as would cripple the working of an organization elsewhere, becomes the source of strength and blessing in the Spiritual Assembly whose members, far from dwelling on their differences in education, capacity and ability, can work together in accordance with the spirit of Bahá'u'lláh's Administrative Order to create a loving and harmonious body pulsating with the spirit of the Cause and demonstrating thereby the dynamism of its cohesive power.

The Role of the Individual

Using the previous analogy in which Spiritual Assemblies are likened to channels carrying the water of life, each member could be compared to one of the bricks which compose that channel. Let us build a channel with nine bricks, each different in size and shape, and then examine the strains and stresses within it as the water passes through.

Should the nine stones be cemented together in such a way that their smooth sides are placed inside the channel, then the water can flow freely. But if some stones stand out in the way of the stream the result will be turbulence. Every brick will be subjected to great pres-

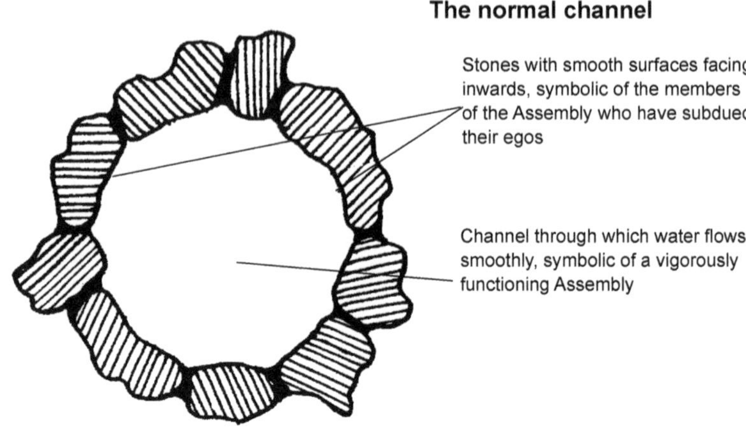

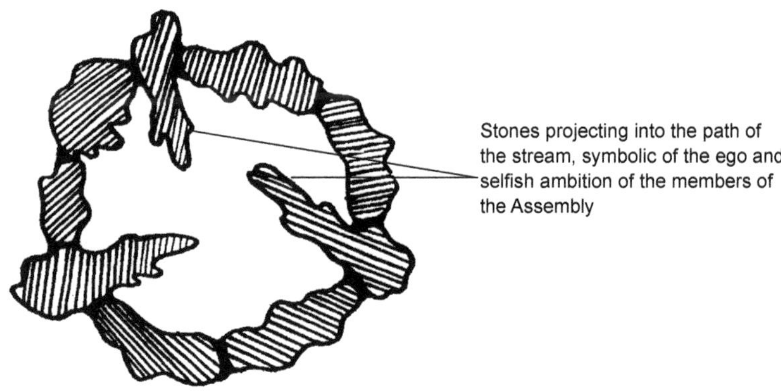

sures so that, in the end, the channel may be destroyed. Similarly, if the members of a Spiritual Assembly meet together in a spirit of harmony and unity, eliminate their selfish desires, leave behind their egos and are, through their love for Bahá'u'lláh, merged and fused into one body, then this Assembly becomes spiritual. It will attract the bounties of Bahá'u'lláh and through it the spirit and power of the teachings will flow to humanity. But should members bring with them their sense of superiority and pride in their own accomplishments and thereby raise their egos so that they protrude like the stones in the channel, then that Assembly, in the words of 'Abdu'l-Bahá, will be 'brought to naught'.[12] The Assembly will become the centre of turbulence and the channel bearing the spirit of the Cause may be completely clogged. There will be a period of intense pain, of suffering and tension in the Assembly. Those who suffer most are often the very people who have raised their egos. The mighty forces of the Faith flowing through the institution will exert great pressure on these obstacles and, in the same way that the stones which protrude into the channel are hit by the stream and are eventually washed away, so the Administrative Order does not harbour vain and egotistical personalities. It calls for humility and self-effacement, for servitude and detachment. The standard it demands from every member of the Assembly is epitomized by the following words of the Master where He exhorts the believers to tread the path of humility and servitude: 'Make me as dust in the pathway of Thy loved ones . . .'[13] Bahá'u'lláh, in many of His Tablets, has extolled humility and servitude as the greatest station destined for a human being. Not until the individual acquires these virtues can one's deed, however meritorious, become acceptable to God. Let us consider, for instance, what the most acceptable gift is that one can give to a friend. It will be an article which the friend does not already possess. Then what is it that one can offer to God that will be acceptable to Him? God possesses everything. A person's accomplishments, knowledge, virtue, wealth and power if offered to God at the end of a lifetime are as utter nothingness when compared with God's transcendent glory. Yet, by virtue of His sovereignty and dominion, humility is not one of His attributes and, therefore, in His sight this is the most acceptable gift a person can give. Humility and servitude before the believers are the two essential qualities for members of Spiritual Assemblies. Without them the spirit of love and unity which must exist at the time of consultation will be destroyed and the Assembly will not be able to function in accordance with the spirit of the Administrative Order.

Influences of the Old Order

Other harmful elements that may be introduced into the nascent institutions of the Faith are the evil influences of the old order which has been breaking up ever since Bahá'u'lláh's summons to the kings and rulers went unheeded. The bearers of these harmful influences are the believers who have to live and work in the outside world – a world encircled by the gloom of unbelief and godlessness, spiritually famished, full of corruption, prejudice and strife, with its false standards and its hollow and outworn institutions functioning for the most part within a framework based on intrigues, deception and discord. The believers, however sincere, can unwittingly bring with them into the Assembly, if they are not ever watchful, some of the standards and practices of the old order, so alien to the spirit of the Faith and its divinely ordained institutions.

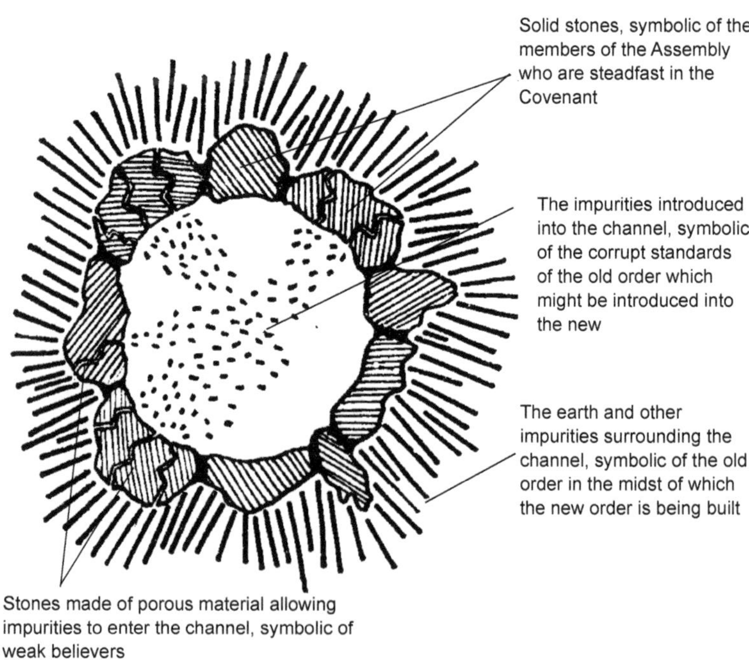

Let us consider the analogy of the channel made up of nine bricks. Though pure water flows within it, the channel itself is surrounded by, and buried within, the earth. Should any one of those bricks be made of porous material, it will allow some of the impurities from the outside to pass into the channel and the water will become contaminated with soil and dirt. But if the bricks are strong, solid and impregnable, nothing from the outside can seep through and the water within the channel will remain pure and unpolluted. This is true of the members of the Spiritual Assembly. The individual members' strength, solidarity and firmness are dependent upon having faith in Bahá'u'lláh and obedience to His commandments. A lukewarm and fainthearted believer whose faith in Bahá'u'lláh is not wholehearted is likely to become influenced by those loose standards, the decadent theories and the corrupt practices of a rapidly declining order and become the means of introducing some of its unwholesome elements into the nascent institutions of Bahá'u'lláh's world-embracing Faith.

The Faith of Bahá'u'lláh stands far above the fears, doubts and perplexities of the old and outworn institutions and obsolescent doctrines, whether social, political or religious, and is in no way influenced by the fabricated, the hollow and the godless philosophies and theories which have been promulgated in modern times and which have miserably failed to produce an acceptable solution for the problems facing humanity. Those members of the Assembly, however, who have recognized the station of Bahá'u'lláh and are steadfast in His Covenant are safe from the poisonous influences of the old order. Through their staunch faith in Bahá'u'lláh, their undeviating loyalty to 'Abdu'l-Bahá, Shoghi Effendi and the Universal House of Justice, their rectitude of conduct, their unfailing adherence to the laws, teachings and ordinances of Bahá'u'lláh, these members are armed against, and protected from, the evil influences that exert pressure upon the newly-born divine institutions. In the channel of the Administrative Order these souls are indeed as solid and impregnable stones.

Steadfastness in the Covenant

Faith is a relative term and its intensity varies from person to person. When the individual recognizes for the first time the truth of Bahá'u'lláh's mission, the spark of faith is ignited in the heart. This spark will grow into a mighty flame if one allows the love of Bahá'u'lláh to enter into one's heart, arises to serve His Cause and be immersed in the ocean of His words. Only in this way will the heart receive an ever-increasing measure of confirmation and assurance.

No story of the early believers is more moving than that of the martyrs of the Faith who, fearlessly and with great heroism, arose in the propagation of the Cause of God and who remained steadfast until, in the end, they testified with their life-blood to the truth of the Revelation of Bahá'u'lláh. These souls attained the highest degree of faith and were the embodiments of certitude and assurance. A story of great inspiration recorded in the annals of the Faith is that of Rúḥu'lláh Varqá, a teenage martyr of the Faith, a hero and indeed a spiritual prodigy. It was he who, at the age of eight, attained the presence of Bahá'u'lláh in 'Akká and through his love for the Blessed Beauty demonstrated such maturity and understanding that the believers were inspired and uplifted by him and felt the greatness of his soul. His devotion to the Cause and enthusiasm for its propagation carried him, soon after attaining the presence of His Lord, to the prison of Ṭihrán where he shared with his illustrious father, the outstanding poet and teacher of the Faith 'Alí-Muḥammad (an Apostle of Bahá'u'lláh, surnamed Varqá [Dove] by the Pen of the Most High), the ordeals and sufferings of prison life. It was in that prison that he witnessed with his own eyes the body of his beloved father fall by the executioner's dagger. He, a short time later, refusing to recant his faith and wishing to join his father, was strangled to death at the age of twelve.

'Abdu'l-Bahá and the Greatest Holy Leaf had a great admiration and love for Rúḥu'lláh and both used to enjoy talking to him when he was in 'Akká. A story told about him is that one day 'Abdu'l-Bahá asked Rúḥu'lláh how he spent his time at home. He replied, 'We teach the Faith to people and tell them of the coming of the Promised One.' The Master, obviously enjoying talking to this wonderful youth and wishing to try him, asked what he would do if it were found that the Báb was not the true Promised One and that the real prophet had appeared. 'I shall teach him the Faith,' was his prompt reply. This is an example of true faith, of absolute certitude and steadfastness in the Covenant.

Though the Heroic Age has ended, the believers in the Formative Age are tested in different ways. One such testing ground is at the meeting of the Spiritual Assembly where the individual member will be tested in thought, word and deed and where his qualities and potential will become known. The best protection for the believers is steadfastness in the Covenant which, in simple language, means obedience to Bahá'u'lláh and, after Him, to 'Abdu'l-Bahá, Shoghi Effendi and, today, to the Universal House of Justice. This is a matter of faith and every Bahá'í who has recognized Bahá'u'lláh as the Supreme Manifestation of God will already have accepted this cardinal principle of the Cause.

There are many teachings or principles in the Faith with which a person may agree. The faith of a believer is tested, however, when one comes across a statement which is contrary to one's way of thinking. In this instance it may be said that the degree of steadfastness in the Covenant is determined by the ready manner in which one acknowledges, sincerely and from the heart, that Bahá'u'lláh and those upon whom He has conferred infallibility are divinely guided, that their words, their teachings and their guidance are free from error and that the human mind is finite and one's judgements often erroneous.

Spiritual Standards

A great responsibility that falls on the shoulders of those who are called upon to serve on Spiritual Assemblies is to ensure that the administrative principles revealed by the pen of Bahá'u'lláh, elaborated by 'Abdu'l-Bahá and explained in detail by Shoghi Effendi, are faithfully applied in the working of these institutions.

An important instance of these principles is on the occasion of consultation in the Spiritual Assembly. The standards which, according to Bahá'u'lláh and 'Abdu'l-Bahá, the members of the Spiritual Assemblies must uphold during their consultation are very high indeed. 'The prime requisites for them that take counsel together,' writes 'Abdu'l-Bahá,

> are purity of motive, radiance of spirit, detachment from all else save God, attraction to His Divine Fragrances, humility and lowliness amongst His loved ones, patience and long-suffering in difficulties and servitude to His exalted Threshold.[14]

> The first condition is absolute love and harmony amongst the members of the assembly. They must be wholly free from estrangement and must manifest in themselves the Unity of God, for they are the waves of one sea, the drops of one river, the stars of one heaven, the rays of one sun, the trees of one orchard, the flowers of one garden.[15]

It is the application of these spiritual standards that makes Bahá'í consultation a testing ground for every member of the Assembly. All the virtues of the individual, his faith, his courage and his steadfastness in the Covenant, undergo a rigorous test as the members of the Assembly sit around the table to consult. Here the spiritual battle within the soul of the individual begins and will continue as long as the ego is the dictator. Indeed, in many cases this battle may last a lifetime. In this battlefield the forces of light and darkness are arrayed against each other. On the one side stands the spiritual entity, the soul of the believer, on the other a great enemy, the self or ego.

The spiritual standard is carried aloft by the Master and should one turn one's heart to the Realm of Glory one can unmistakably hear, with the ears of the spirit, at every Assembly meeting the vibrant voice of the Master summoning us to

'purity of motive'
'radiance of spirit'
'detachment'
'attraction to His Divine Fragrances'
'humility' 'amongst His loved ones'
'patience and long-suffering in difficulties'
'servitude'
'love'
'harmony'
'devotion'
'courtesy'
'dignity'
'care'
'moderation'
'free from estrangement'.[16]

These and many more such attributes are the prime requisites of Bahá'í consultation. Whenever the soul hearkens to these lofty standards set by 'Abdu'l-Bahá and, when the occasion demands, applies them during consultation, the ego, defeated, will recede into the background. The soul emerges victorious from this battle and will become radiant with the light of faith and detachment. The application of these spiritual principles, however, must be genuine and not merely superficial. The feelings of love, unity, detachment and harmony must come from the heart. They must not be manifested in an outward form only. Humility and servitude, radiance, devotion, courtesy and patience, along with all the other virtues, are qualities of the spirit. These cannot be manifested by paying lip service to them. If this is the case then the ego is victor.

Presence of Bahá'u'lláh

It may not be easy for anyone to attain to such lofty standards during Bahá'í consultation. No matter how sincere and devoted, the members often fail to apply these principles at Assembly meetings. But within the Spiritual Assembly there is a mighty force, often overlooked, which is capable of transforming human failures and shortcomings into noble aspirations and praiseworthy actions. It can change the atmosphere of the Spiritual Assembly from one of tension and discord into one of love and unity. Freed from the entanglement of argument and controversy, the Assembly can then become the perfect channel for the outpouring of the spirit of the Cause to mankind. This potent force is the presence of Bahá'u'lláh in the Assembly. In the Kitáb-i-Aqdas He has stated that when the members assemble in the council chamber they should regard themselves as being in the presence of God, which is indeed the presence of Bahá'u'lláh.

This presence is real and not imaginary, for He calls on the members not only to consider themselves in His presence but to behold 'Him Who is the Unseen'.[17]

In this life things that are real are often not seen with the human eye. This contingent world, and all that can be seen within it, is but a shadow. The world of reality is spiritual, and for its comprehension people need spiritual qualities. The presence of Bahá'u'lláh in the Spiritual Assembly is more real than anything else within that body and, as the members assemble, they are indeed seated in His presence as He Himself has affirmed. When the members of the Assembly become truly conscious of this and, with the eye of the spirit, see Bahá'u'lláh in their midst, they will be immersed in the ocean of humility and self-effacement, will be filled with a new spirit and will become radiant. The presence of Bahá'u'lláh will fuse the nine members into one body and they will no longer dwell on the faults and shortcomings of one another. Every word that a member utters, every idea that one puts forward, every contribution that one makes during consultation will, in reality, be addressed to Bahá'u'lláh in a spirit of humility and servitude. Within such an atmosphere Bahá'í consultation becomes truly constructive, for no member can help but offer ideas frankly and cordially.

The inhibitions which could often prevent one member from expressing personal views, for various reasons, such as the possibility of becoming unpopular within the community or offending other members of the Assembly, will disappear and be replaced by courage and wisdom. Indeed, in this instance, when the individual turns to Bahá'u'lláh with a pure motive, the words uttered will produce such an effect on the hearers that no one will be offended.

The consciousness of the presence of Bahá'u'lláh in the Assembly will create a spiritual atmosphere, souls will become humble, any feelings of superiority will vanish and the ego will be swept aside. For, in the presence of Bahá'u'lláh, who could consider oneself superior to one's fellow members? Who would belittle the opinion of another, whether outwardly or in one's heart? Who would lose his temper, raise his voice, interrupt or argue with his friend in the Assembly, or who would adopt an attitude, or speak in a way, that could offend another soul?

True Consultation

A Spiritual Assembly that functions in this way is 'in truth, appointed of God'.[18] 'O ye who are firm in the Covenant' are the assuring words with which the Master addresses the members of Spiritual Assemblies,

> 'Abdu'l-Bahá is constantly engaged in ideal communication with any Spiritual Assembly which is instituted through the divine bounty, and the members of which, in the utmost devotion, turn to the divine Kingdom and are firm in the Covenant. To them He is whole-heartedly attached and with them He is linked by everlasting ties.[19]

Bahá'í consultation that is carried out in accordance with the spirit of the Administrative Order is a creative process whereby different opinions and ideas develop into a well-balanced and mature decision. The members of the Assembly have first to familiarize themselves with the facts relating to the subject under consideration and then, in a prayerful attitude, express their views and opinions frankly and candidly.

'In this Cause,' 'Abdu'l-Bahá states,

> consultation is of vital importance, but spiritual conference and not mere voicing of personal views is intended . . .
>
> The purpose is to emphasize the statement that consultation must have for its object the investigation of truth . . . Man should weigh his opinions with the utmost sincerity, calmness and composure. Before expressing his own views he should carefully consider the views already advanced by others. If he finds that a previously expressed opinion is more true and worthy, he should accept it immediately and not wilfully hold to an opinion of his own . . . Therefore true consultation is spiritual conference in the attitude and atmosphere of love. Members must love each other in the spirit of fellowship in order that good results may be forthcoming. Love and fellowship are the foundation.[20]

Often an idea put forward by one member stimulates other ideas and these flow from one to another until they become crystallized in the form of a resolution, which is the child of Bahá'í consultation and is unanimously carried. In other cases, when a resolution is carried by a majority decision, it is no less valid and all members support it wholeheartedly for the simple reason that 'Abdu'l-Bahá has enjoined on the believers to do so. This is one of the spiritual principles that govern the workings of the Administrative Order. If this support is not given from the heart, then the individual has not acted in accordance with the spirit of the Faith.

No member of an Assembly who has been true to the tenets of the Faith and has progressed spiritually would harbour in his mind the thought of giving himself any credit for his suggestions or ideas, no matter how meritorious these might be. To be opinionated, dogmatic, stubborn and argumentative in Bahá'í consultation is to oppose the very spirit of the Faith. The practices of dictation of ideas, of lobbying and persuasion, so often employed within the institutions of the old order, are contrary to the teachings of Bahá'u'lláh.

No Compromise on Principles

In their eagerness to solve a problem to the satisfaction of all or their anxiety not to offend the feelings of particular individuals or the community as a whole, members of a Spiritual Assembly may, sometimes unconsciously or even instinctively, reach a decision based on compromising a basic principle. This is another harmful influence of the old order which can undoubtedly damage the working of the Spiritual Assembly. Whereas the non-Bahá'í institutions, whether social, political or religious, often turn to compromise as an effective instrument for the solution of their problems, the embryonic institutions of the new World Order draw their strength and vigour from the truth of the word of God revealed by Bahá'u'lláh.

The laws, the principles and the teachings which 40 years of continuous Revelation have vouchsafed to humanity and which must govern the workings of these institutions for a period of no less than a thousand years are all clear and explicit and subject to no alteration or compromise. In addition, during the 29 years of His ministry 'Abdu'l-Bahá disclosed the inner spirit of these teachings and elucidated their meaning. This was followed by 36 years of Guardianship during which Shoghi Effendi, through his communications with individuals as well as Assemblies, not only amplified the interpretations of 'Abdu'l-Bahá but also applied most of these laws and principles to specific cases. Though members of Spiritual Assemblies are free to exercise their right of self-expression and to take their own initiative during the Assembly's deliberations and though they have plenty of scope to consult and reach decisions on matters that fall within their jurisdiction, they are, nevertheless, obliged to follow the guidance of Bahá'u'lláh, 'Abdu'l-Bahá, Shoghi Effendi and the Universal House of Justice and to apply this to their own particular circumstances without any compromise. Indeed, this vast ocean of divine guidance will give clear orientation to Bahá'í consultation at every Assembly meeting, enabling the members to avoid many pitfalls and to reach decisions which are in accordance with the spirit of the Faith.

Administrative Principles

One of the unique features of the Faith is that Bahá'u'lláh has revealed a new range of teachings which are unprecedented in the older Dispensations and are designed to regulate the functioning of the administrative institutions of His Cause. During the entire period of the Prophetic Cycle, beginning with Adam and ending with Muḥammad, and even during the Bábí Dispensation, the scope and the application of spiritual teachings remained almost the same. The Sermon on the Mount, epitomizing the spiritual and moral teachings of Christianity, might be regarded as the basic pattern and essence of spiritual teachings in all religions. These spiritual teachings have exerted a deep and ever-abiding influence on people's lives and actions. Neither the passage of time, nor even the fact that the former religions are no longer able to cope with the problems of this age, have been effective in erasing from the hearts of people some eternal spiritual teachings with which they were brought up and which have been so ingrained in their minds and souls as to become almost second nature to them. So profound has been this influence that even among those who have become disillusioned, lost their faith and joined the ranks of agnostics and atheists many are found who are driven by their consciences to practise these humanitarian and spiritual principles as a way of life.

Never before, until the advent of the Bahá'í Dispensation, did a Manifestation of God and the Centre of His Covenant so widen the range of these spiritual teachings as to include a series of administrative principles designed to govern the workings of the institutions of His new World Order. The spiritual and administrative principles have been placed on a par with each other and are accorded equal importance. Therefore, in this age not only must the believers follow the basic spiritual teachings of love, honesty, forgiveness and all other divine commandments which are primarily intended for individuals in their relationships with each other, but they must also observe these principles which define their role within Bahá'í society and which determine a person's conduct in relation to its institutions.

The strength and effectiveness of the institutions of the embryonic World Order of Bahá'u'lláh are not due only to their divine origin and to the spirit of the Faith which flows through them but also to the fact that the believers observe the administrative principles as an act of faith, that they obey wholeheartedly the commandments of Bahá'u'lláh in relation to these institutions and that, in the performance of their administrative duties, they vigilantly guard against the introduction into the Administrative Order of any unwholesome element which would tend to hamper its growth, sap its strength or debase its station.

Election

To enumerate a few administrative principles let us first consider the election of the Spiritual Assembly. Although an administrative function, the election of the Spiritual Assembly has a great spiritual significance and is to be carried out in a spirit of prayer and devotion. The Guardian has indicated the qualifications of the members of an Assembly. The elector, when voting for them, should

> . . . consider without the least trace of passion and prejudice, and irrespective of any material consideration, the names of only those who can best combine the necessary qualities of unquestioned loyalty, of selfless devotion, of a well-trained mind, of recognized ability and mature experience.[21]

In Bahá'í elections there is to be no electioneering, canvassing or propaganda. Such practices are against the spirit of the Cause of Bahá'u'lláh and are clearly forbidden. The electors have freedom of choice and the election is by secret ballot. It is improper for two people, even a husband and wife, to consult together or to influence each other in their choice. These administrative principles are sacred to a Bahá'í and to break them is tantamount to breaking a spiritual principle.

Authority of the Institutions

Another important administrative principle is to accept the decisions of the Spiritual Assembly even if these decisions prove to be wrong. The Spiritual Assemblies are not infallible bodies but if the members of the Assembly, regardless of their personal views, support its decisions wholeheartedly the truth will be manifested and the Assembly will be led to correct a previous decision. Even if this does occur, the pattern of the Administrative Order is such that a wrong decision can be righted. Local Assemblies are linked to their National Assemblies and these in turn to the Universal House of Justice. The National Assembly, by virtue of its wider jurisdiction and authority over the Local Assemblies within its province, is in a better position to draw the attention of the Local Assembly to a resolution which it considers to be wrong and to ask that body to reconsider its decision. If need be, the Universal House of Justice may, in the end, give its final and infallible verdict on the subject.

The authority with which Bahá'u'lláh, 'Abdu'l-Bahá and Shoghi Effendi have invested both Local and National Assemblies is clear and unquestionable. It is enjoined upon the believers to obey the decisions of their Assembly. To disobey them on the grounds that a decision might be wrong is not permitted.

Shoghi Effendi has clearly stated the authority of the National Assembly in these words:

> I wish to reaffirm in clear and categorical language, the principle already enunciated upholding the supreme authority of the National Assembly in all matters that affect the interest of the Faith . . . There can be no conflict of authority, no duality under any form or circumstances in any sphere of Bahá'í jurisdiction whether local, national, or international. The National Assembly, however, although the sole interpreter of its Declaration of Trust and By-Laws, is directly and morally responsible if it allows any body or institution within its jurisdiction to abuse its privileges or to decline in the exercise

> of its rights and prerogatives. It is the trusted guardian and the mainspring of the manifold activities and interests of every national community in the Bahá'í world. It constitutes the sole link that binds these communities to the International House of Justice, the supreme administrative body in the Dispensation of Bahá'u'lláh.[22]

Although the Spiritual Assembly has been given authority to deal with matters that fall within its jurisdiction and is empowered to enforce its decisions whenever the situation demands it, and despite the fact that its members are not answerable for their actions to those who have elected them, notwithstanding this, the Assembly is not an institution whose members act with dictatorial powers. On the contrary, every matter that comes up at the Assembly meeting is to be dealt with in a spirit of loving consultation, care and justice.

Responsibility of Members

The Guardian has described the attitude and responsibilities of the members of the Spiritual Assembly in these words:

> Their [i.e. the members of the Assembly] function is not to dictate, but to consult, and consult not only among themselves, but as much as possible with the Friends whom they represent. They must regard themselves in no other light but that of chosen instruments for a more efficient and dignified presentation of the Cause of God. They should never be led to suppose that they are the central ornaments of the body of the Cause, intrinsically superior to others in capacity or merit, and sole promoters of its teachings and principles. They should approach their task with extreme humility, and endeavour, by their open-mindedness, their high sense of justice and duty, their candour, their modesty, their entire devotion to the welfare and interests of the Friends, the Cause, and humanity, to win, not only the confidence and the genuine support and respect of those whom they serve, but

> also their esteem and real affection. They must, at all times, avoid the spirit of exclusiveness, the atmosphere of secrecy, free themselves from a domineering attitude, and banish all forms of prejudice and passion from their deliberations. They should, within the limits of wise discretion, take the Friends into their confidence, acquaint them with their plans, share with them their problems and anxieties, and seek their advice and counsel. And, when they are called upon to arrive at a certain decision, they should, after dispassionate, anxious, and cordial consultation, turn to God in prayer, and with earnestness and conviction and courage record their vote and abide by the voice of the majority, which we are told by our Master to be the voice of truth, never to be challenged, and always to be wholeheartedly enforced. To this voice the Friends must heartily respond, and regard it as the only means that can ensure the protection and advancement of the Cause.[23]

Whereas it is easy to accept and obey a decision with which one agrees, it is not always easy to do so when one does not agree and considers the decision to be wrong, especially if it relates to a problem in which one is personally involved. This is one of the tests that confront the believers in this age and is, in effect, a spiritual battle which many individuals have to fight in order to acquire spiritual qualities, to draw nearer to Bahá'u'lláh and to become detached from earthly things.

Detachment

It is often attachment to this world that clouds the vision and makes the individual proud, arrogant and self-centred. Obedience to Bahá'u'lláh, humility and submissiveness towards the institutions will, in the end, confer inestimable blessings upon the soul.

Attachment to this world is often mistakenly understood to be the possession of earthly goods. 'Should a man,' Bahá'u'lláh explains to His followers, 'wish to adorn himself with the ornaments of the earth, to wear its apparels, or partake of the benefits it can bestow, no harm can befall him, if he alloweth nothing whatever to intervene between him and God, for God hath ordained every good thing, whether created in the heavens or in the earth, for such of His servants as truly believe in Him.'[24]

There is a story in Persian that throws some light on the nature and meaning of detachment from this world. It is the story of a king and a dervish.[25] The king had many spiritual qualities but in his heart he envied the dervish who seemed to have no attachment to this world. For all that a dervish possessed was a basket in which he carried his food. He spent his time roaming around town chanting the praises of his Lord and having mystical communion with Him. He had no home and no belongings yet he considered himself to be so rich that he owned the whole world. To this way of life the king was attracted, so he invited a dervish to his palace in order to learn some lessons in detachment. The dervish came and stayed for some time. At last the king decided to give up his throne and live the life of a dervish. Putting on some old clothes, he disguised himself as a poor man and left his palace with his guest.

They had walked together some distance when the dervish realized that he had left his basket behind in the palace. He explained to the king that they had better go back and fetch it. It was by this incident that the dervish was finally tested and found to be attached to this world. The king had left behind his palaces and his treasures and was treading the path of detachment, whereas the dervish preaching this very virtue for a lifetime proved in the end to be attached to his small basket.

Attachment is an attitude of mind and is not necessarily related to riches. The pride which the individual may have in being learned and knowledgeable, one's accomplishments in this life, position in the community, fame and popularity, the love of one's own self and earthly possessions could all become barriers between the soul and God.

Unity

Another principle that plays an important role in the proper functioning of the Spiritual Assembly is the unity of its members. Unity should not be taken as uniformity or having the same views and ideas during consultation. On the contrary, as 'Abdu'l-Bahá has explained, 'the shining spark of truth cometh forth only after the clash of differing opinions'.[26] By unity is meant a spiritual tie that binds the members together and which derives its cohesive force from Bahá'u'lláh. The key to achieving this unity is to love the other members with the love of God and not for their own sakes, and to look at their perfections, not their shortcomings. To prefer oneself above other members and to belittle their opinions, no matter how immature or inadequate these might be, is against the spirit of the teachings of Bahá'u'lláh and is indicative of immaturity and egotism on the part of the individual concerned.

Justice and Love

When the heart is deprived of faith and belief in God the individual tends to be motivated by animal nature. It is then that, instead of looking upon others with the eye of compassion, one views them with the eye of justice, finds many faults in them and passes judgement upon them. On the other hand, the institutions of the old order, whose main function is supposed to be maintenance of law and order and peace within society, incline more and more towards leniency, forgiveness and compassion instead of firmness, justice and equity.

The Faith of Bahá'u'lláh, through the dynamic influence it exerts on the hearts of men, aims to reverse this pattern within human society. It teaches that it is not for an individual to judge others or to look upon them with the eye of criticism. It clearly asserts that the relationship of one individual with another is based on love and compassion and that to forgive and to have a sin-covering eye is a praiseworthy virtue as far as the individual is concerned. It proclaims, however, that the basis upon which the Spiritual Assemblies

– the institutions which, in the fullness of time, will evolve into Houses of Justice – are established is not forgiveness but justice. The following is an extract from a letter written on behalf of the Guardian:

> He, like the Master before him, is so anxious to see the Believers united in serving the Faith. If between the Friends, true love – based on the love of God – could become manifest, the Cause would spread very rapidly. Love is the standard which must govern the conduct of one believer towards another. The administrative order does not change this, but unfortunately sometimes the friends confuse the two, and try to be a whole spiritual assembly – with the discipline and justice and impartiality that body must show – to each other, instead of being forgiving, loving and patient to each other as individuals.[27]

Supporting Assembly Decisions

A further principle that protects the institutions of the Faith from yet another evil deeply rooted within the fabric of present-day society is embodied in the commandment of 'Abdu'l-Bahá forbidding the believers to 'object to or censure, whether in or out of the meeting',[28] the decisions of the Spiritual Assembly. In a world afflicted by much trouble and unrest, where men and women from all walks of life, individually and collectively, raise their voices in protest against the actions of the authorities, whether religious or political, and at times resort to violence in order to force their views on them, the followers of Bahá'u'lláh are not influenced by the vain disputes, the transient passions, the controversies and the entanglements which surround them within the old order; for they are so filled with the spirit of the Faith of Bahá'u'lláh that they obey this commandment of 'Abdu'l-Bahá with the utmost sincerity. A true Bahá'í, therefore, will not criticize or censure the decisions of the Spiritual Assembly in word or attitude. A member of the Spiritual Assembly who does not wholeheartedly accept the majority decision of the Assembly is indeed breaking a spiritual commandment of the Cause of God. At the same time, the individual is not deprived of the right to air personal views through proper channels and, if dissatisfied, to appeal against a decision of the Assembly. The believer is given ample opportunity to raise any matters with the Spiritual Assembly, either personally or in consultation with the community at the Nineteen Day Feast, and has the right of appeal to the National Spiritual Assembly against a decision of the Local Assembly, or to the Universal House of Justice against that of the National Spiritual Assembly. But, in the meantime, the individual will continue to accept the decision of the Assembly until the result of the appeal is made known. To challenge the authority of the Assembly at any time or for any reason is to break yet another spiritual principle firmly established in the Cause of God.

The Bounty of Serving on the Assembly

Service on the Spiritual Assembly is a great bounty that Bahá'u'lláh has bestowed on His loved ones. It confers upon the individual member not only the unique privilege of taking part in the erection of the framework of His World Order but also enables one to improve one's character and to acquire spiritual qualities through the spiritual battles one must fight in order to subdue one's self and passion during the periods of Bahá'í consultation.

Let us once more refer to the analogy of the channel with nine bricks. As a result of the water flowing through, the bricks inside the channel will, after some time, lose their roughness and sharp edges. Similarly the individual's shortcomings and weaknesses will come to the surface at Assembly meetings and will take their stand against the onrushing forces of the spirit of the Cause flowing through. By this interaction, ignorance, prejudice and other human failings will gradually be diminished and will be replaced by a greater measure of maturity and wisdom.

Balance Between Form and Spirit

Membership of the Spiritual Assembly carries with it great responsibilities too. A major responsibility that falls on the shoulders of the Assembly members is to ensure that the affairs of the Assembly are conducted in accordance with the spiritual and administrative principles laid down by the Central Figures of the Faith and not after the pattern of man-made theories borrowed from the outside world.

The Administrative Order of Bahá'u'lláh consists of two parts: the form and the spirit. The relationship of the two is like that of the body and the soul. Although the essential part is the soul, it does not mean that the body should be neglected. It is important to preserve the balance between the two. An essential aspect of the form of the Administrative Order which it is necessary for the Spiritual Assemblies to develop in their own ways is a system of administration based on efficiency and order. But administrative procedures and systems should only be considered as a means to an end and not the ultimate purpose, which is the flow of the spirit of the Cause through the embryonic institutions of Bahá'u'lláh's World Order.

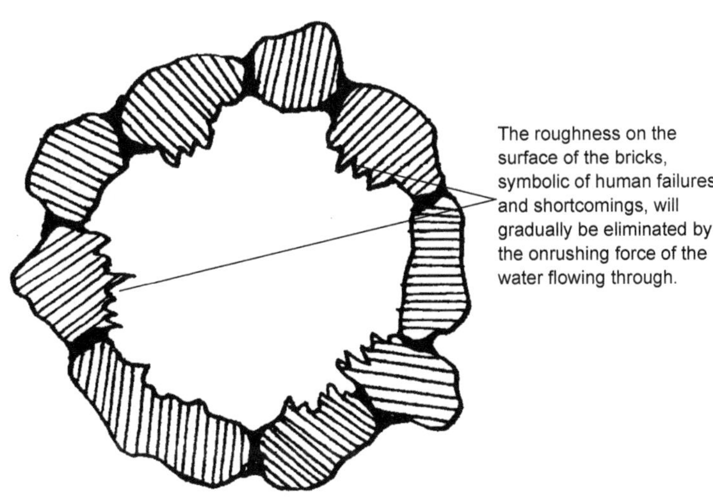

It is the responsibility of each member of the Assembly to guard against attempting to perfect the administrative machinery at the risk of losing the spirit and so creating a situation in which the Assembly, over a period of time, may be moulded into a rigid form, efficient in administration but enslaved by rules and regulations, highly organized yet devoid of the spirit of love and cooperation which are the distinguishing features of the new World Order.

The Institution of the Hands of the Cause and Counsellors

As the Administrative Order of Bahá'u'lláh unfolds, some of its unique features are gradually being revealed and the pattern of the development of its institutions is becoming more evident with the passage of time. One such feature is the manner in which the healthy functioning of Spiritual Assemblies, both local and national, are to be safeguarded. This responsibility falls not only on the members of the Local and National Assemblies but also on an institution which plays an important role in, and constitutes a vital part of, the Administrative Order, namely, the institution of the Hands of the Cause of God.

This institution and the Boards of Counsellors – this latter perpetuating into the future two of the functions of the Hands of the Cause, the protection and propagation of the Faith – have come into being by means of appointment and not by election. Power and authority are invested solely in the Local and National Spiritual Assemblies and the direction of the affairs of the Cause in their respective areas is entrusted to them. The Counsellors are not administrators and their function is not, therefore, to administer the affairs of the Faith but rather, through their counsels and advice to the National Assemblies, through the loving care and assistance which they, together with their Board members, extend to the Local Assemblies, and by inspiring the believers and encouraging them in the discharge of their administrative duties, this body plays a major role in the protection of the Faith and the healthy functioning of the institutions of Bahá'u'lláh's embryonic World Order.

Before the appointment by Shoghi Effendi in 1951 of the

first contingent of living Hands of the Cause since the time of Bahá'u'lláh, the Spiritual Assemblies were the only bodies that handled the manifold affairs of the community. But with the creation of this second arm, which later was reinforced by the appointment of the Continental Boards of Counsellors by the Universal House of Justice, the manner in which the Spiritual Assemblies were to discharge their responsibilities was considerably changed. The time for the Spiritual Assemblies to undertake their obligations singlehandedly has passed. Today no Spiritual Assembly, whether local or national, can function properly unless and until it fully incorporates in its activities the assistance of the second arm of the Administrative Order which performs a vital function in the healthy operation of Local and National Spiritual Assemblies as well as enhancing the spiritual well-being of the Bahá'í community.

The two arms of the Administrative Order function independently and in the course of their activities do not interfere with each other. This is similar to the arms of the human body. Each arm is activated independently. The right arm does not control the movement of the left and vice versa. They are activated separately but come together when lifting a weight. However, there are some functions that the two institutions might carry out independently of each other. For example, in the above analogy, when one hand is writing, the other hand should not come to assist. If it does, this is interference.

At this time in the development of the Administrative Order the Continental Boards of Counsellors consult and cooperate with National Spiritual Assemblies while the Auxiliary Board members and their assistants consult with Local Spiritual Assemblies. The Counsellors, their Auxiliary Board members and assistants constitute one arm of the Administrative Order, and the National Spiritual Assemblies and their committees the other arm. When these two institutions in a country cooperate and support each other in a spirit of unity, great powers are released to the community which will, in turn, strengthen the foundation of the institutions of the Faith and accelerate its progress in that region.

Healthy Functioning of Spiritual Assemblies

The institutions of the Local and National Spiritual Assemblies grow and develop in the same manner as any living organism that grows organically. These divine institutions go through a process of maturation that will continue for a long time during the Formative Age of the Faith. At present, however, the Spiritual Assemblies are in their stages of infancy and childhood and consequently cannot be expected to function as mature bodies. Although the members of a Spiritual Assembly may be very mature and devoted Bahá'ís, the institution itself is young and immature. It is important to note that there is a vast difference between Bahá'í and non-Bahá'í organizations. There are many institutions in the world that work to perfection like machines but are devoid of spirit. In contrast to this, the Bahá'í Spiritual Assemblies, though immature at present, are pulsating with life, are full of spirit and have the promise of the future when they are destined to evolve into mighty institutions endowed with the capacity to guide and direct the affairs of the community in the best possible manner.

In these days when Spiritual Assemblies are in their infancy, the believers treat them with respect and obey them even if their decisions be wrong and full of shortcomings, knowing that only the passage of time will bring maturity to these divinely-ordained institutions. This attitude of cherishing and supporting the Spiritual Assemblies is similar to the way in which parents treat their children. A child by its nature can disturb the surroundings of his house but the parents know that the child cannot be expected to act as an adult. Thus they are not concerned about his behaviour because they know in the future when he grows up he will cease to act in a childish way and will behave in a responsible manner.

Although the Spiritual Assemblies at this stage of their development are bound to be weak and inexperienced, this weakness should not be regarded as a licence for the members of these institutions to become heedless of their vital responsibilities. In the above analogy, one does not expect a child to be faultless in his actions but he should be healthy. It is the same with Spiritual Assemblies functioning at the present time. It is not expected of them not to make mistakes in their deliberations but the members are exhorted by the Master to love one another in their innermost hearts. Of course, it is easy to love a person whom one likes. However, the challenge is to love those with whom one finds it difficult to work.

In the last analysis, however, the vigour and vitality of an Assembly devolves upon its members, for it is through their sincerity and devotion to the Faith that all the high ideals and principles laid down by the Blessed Beauty and the Centre of His Covenant are applied to the work of the Spiritual Assembly. A deeper study of the writings of Shoghi Effendi on Bahá'í Administration will enable the individual to realize that the aim of the members of the Assembly in this period of the Formative Age of the Faith should not primarily be directed towards becoming efficient administrators or specialists in solving the community's various complex problems but rather towards creating a spiritual atmosphere during the course of their meetings, so that the confirmations of Bahá'u'lláh may reach them from every direction and that, through His assistance, they may be able to resolve their problems.

The way in which this can be achieved, as already stated, is through the firmness of one's faith in Bahá'u'lláh and loyalty to His Covenant, through the suppression of the ego and through 'purity of motive . . . humility and lowliness amongst His loved ones . . . and servitude to His exalted Threshold'.[29] This is the challenge that faces the 'trusted ones of the Merciful'[30] in this age.

The New World Order in Embryo

At a time when forces of destruction are sweeping the surface of the earth, plunging the whole of the human race into a state of chaos and dismay and uprooting its time-honoured institutions, the comparatively small community of the Most Great Name, consisting of men and women from all walks of life, young and old, rich and poor, literate and illiterate, armed with the invincible power of faith, strengthened by the unfailing support and confirmations of the Lord of Hosts and confident of ultimate victory, are engaged in erecting the framework of new institutions embracing the whole planet and designed to evolve, in the fullness of time, into a New World Order to be established in the name of Bahá'u'lláh. This World Order which is destined to come into being in the future in the plenitude of its glory and the establishment of which will signalize at once the emergence of the Bahá'í Commonwealth, the hoisting of the banner of the Most Great Peace and the advent of the Kingdom of God on earth, is today growing in its embryonic form and is referred to as the 'Administrative Order'. This Administrative Order has been systematically developing within the Bahá'í community since the inception of the Formative Age.

The Four Charters

'Abdu'l-Bahá has left to posterity His Will and Testament, which may be regarded as the child of the Covenant and the 'Charter of the new World Order'. In it He has delineated the features of the Administrative Order, laid down its principles, defined its functions and called on the Bahá'ís to begin the task of erecting its institutions. Another significant series of Tablets, 14 in all, addressed by 'Abdu'l-Bahá to the American believers – the Tablets of the Divine

Plan – fulfil a major role in the propagation of the Faith among all the nations and peoples of the world and constitute the 'Charter for the teaching of the Faith'[31] throughout the planet. In these Tablets 'Abdu'l-Bahá exhorts Bahá'ís to detach themselves from earthly things, sanctify their souls from the dross of this world, arise in a spirit of love and unity and travel far and wide to every corner of the globe for the advancement of the Cause of God. In these Tablets He also names 120 countries, territories and islands to which Bahá'í teachers should proceed to teach the Message of Bahá'u'lláh and establish His Faith.

These two documents, together with the Kitáb-i-Aqdas, Bahá'u'lláh's Most Holy Book, regarded as the 'Charter of the future world civilization'[32] and the Tablet of Carmel, revealed by Bahá'u'lláh in the vicinity of the cave of Elijah, the Charter for building the World Centre of the Faith, constitute the major instruments that are to guide the Bahá'í institutions as well as inspiring the believers in their common task of building a new World Order for mankind.

Shoghi Effendi: Builder of the Administrative Order

It was Shoghi Effendi who laid the foundations of the Administrative Order and reared its institutions. At first he concentrated on teaching the believers how to build the Local Spiritual Assemblies and how to work within them. For a period of no less than 15 years he devoted his time to the arduous task of teaching the Bahá'ís the principles of Bahá'í Administration. He explained the function, the scope and the ultimate purpose of local and national institutions. He fashioned the Administrative Order by laying the foundations of the Local Spiritual Assemblies on a firm basis and then erecting upon them the National Spiritual Assemblies which today sustain and support the mighty edifice of Bahá'u'lláh's Universal House of Justice.

At the time of the passing of the Master the believers had certain somewhat crude ideas about the Faith and were not sufficiently mature. There was not an adequate sense of community life among them. It was Shoghi Effendi who, through his eloquent translations of the writings of Bahá'u'lláh and 'Abdu'l-Bahá, through his own masterly writings, through his guidance and direction of the affairs of the Local and National Assemblies throughout the world, through his constant encouragement and perseverance over a period of more than three decades, patiently and effectively unveiled the Faith of Bahá'u'lláh to their eyes. He placed in the right perspective everything that the Faith possessed: its founders, its laws, its ordinances, its teachings, its principles and its institutions – these were all placed, as in a jigsaw pattern, in their relative positions. He enabled the believers to acquire a new conception of community life, of unity and solidarity.

In the Heroic Age of the Faith the believers were so attracted to Bahá'u'lláh that they did not pay much attention to anything else. They were in love with Him and were completely intoxicated by the wine of His presence. But now was the time of the building of the new World Order and it was through Shoghi Effendi's endeavours and guidance that the vision of the Bahá'ís widened. They began to appreciate the Faith in a new light and many arose for the building up of local and national institutions throughout the world.

First 15 Years of the Guardianship

During the first 15 years of the Guardianship no less than eight National Spiritual Assemblies were formed and 30 additional sovereign states were brought within the pale of the Faith. Some other outstanding events during this period were:

- the passing of the Greatest Holy Leaf, sister of 'Abdu'l-Bahá, in 1932
- recognition of the independent status of the Faith in Egypt
- the seizure of Bahá'u'lláh's House in Baghdád, which led to the submission of a petition to the League of Nations whose resolution was to uphold the claim of the Bahá'í community to the House

- the teaching exploits of Martha Root culminating in Queen Marie of Rumania's acclamations of the greatness of the message of Bahá'u'lláh and her love for His teachings
- the creation of the International Bahá'í Bureau in Geneva in 1925
- the implementation of the ordinance of Bahá'u'lláh concerning the institution of the Nineteen Day Feast
- the multiplication of organized youth activities
- the enlargement of Bahá'í endowments and properties in the Holy Land, the United States and Persia
- the acquisition of historic sites in Persia
- the formation of International Bahá'í Archives

In the cradle of the Faith where, during this period, the followers of the Most Great Name were still oppressed by the authorities and were subjected to sporadic outbursts of persecution resulting in the martyrdom of many, Shoghi Effendi turned his attention to the institutions of the Faith which by then were functioning throughout the length and breadth of that land. He gave them a special task which assumes a great importance in the Cause, namely, the implementation of some of the laws of the Kitáb-i-Aqdas, the 'warp and woof' of Bahá'u'lláh's World Order. He directed the Spiritual Assemblies in Persia to begin the enforcement of these laws within the Bahá'í community – laws which, although known to the believers in that land, had not previously been fully observed. In the course of his ministry he elaborated a great deal on the application of these laws, elucidated many intricacies and details connected with them, urged the Spiritual Assemblies never to compromise when enforcing the laws and counselled them to uphold the standard of justice and impartiality in all cases. Thus he built up in this particular field a great reservoir of knowledge and experience which will be of great value in the future.

National Teaching Plans

In the United States of America and Canada – the scene of the building of the pattern of the Administrative Order – the institutions of the Faith had grown and developed to a point where the Guardian was able, in 1937, to launch the first Seven Year Plan, an enterprise of great significance which opens the initial phase in the first epoch in the prosecution of the divine mandate conferred on the North American believers by 'Abdu'l-Bahá and which marks a turning point in the history of the Administrative Order of the Faith.

By the time this Plan had been triumphantly completed in 1944, coinciding with the worldwide celebrations of the centenary of the birth of the Faith, the number of Local Spiritual Assemblies in the United States had almost doubled, the number of localities in which Bahá'ís were residing had enormously increased and the nucleus of the institutions of the Faith had been established in every republic of Latin America. This tremendous achievement, together with the completion of the exterior ornamentation of the holiest House of Worship in the Bahá'í world, awakened the Bahá'ís of other lands to the significance of these events in the United States and Canada and opened their eyes to the pattern of systematic expansion and consolidation of the Faith that had developed as a direct consequence of this first historic Plan initiated by the Guardian of the Cause of God and executed by the followers of Bahá'u'lláh in the cradle of the Administrative Order of the Faith.

Such a glorious triumph for the Cause created an upsurge of eagerness and dedication, of confidence and enthusiasm in the hearts of the believers in other lands. They, too, longed to scale loftier heights in the service of the Cause of God.

As each National Assembly reached the point of readiness the Guardian gave his approval and encouragement to the formulation of national Plans mainly designed to increase the number, and consolidate the institution, of Local Spiritual Assemblies and to multiply the Bahá'í centres within their national boundaries and beyond. The first to turn to the Guardian for a Plan was the British community, who were given a Six Year Plan in 1944. Other Plans followed within two to three years. Each had a certain duration and ended either in 1950, the hundredth anniversary of the martyrdom of the Báb, or in 1953, the Holy Year, the centenary of the birth of Bahá'u'lláh's revelation in the Síyáh-Chál of Ṭihrán.

Foremost among these was the second Seven Year Plan of the Bahá'ís of North America, the duration of which marks the second phase of the initial epoch of the Tablets of the Divine Plan. This Plan, which incorporated some major international goals, including the establishment of Local Spiritual Assemblies in ten countries of Western Europe, the formation of three National Assemblies in the Western Hemisphere and the interior ornamentation of the Mashriqu'l-Adhkár in the United States, was successfully accomplished in 1953. Others were the Indian Four and a Half Year Plan followed by a 19 Month Plan, the Persian 45 Month Plan, the Australian Six Year Plan, the Iraqi Three Year Plan, the Egyptian Five Year Plan, the German Five Year Plan, the Canadian Five Year Plan – which could be regarded as the continuation of the second Seven Year Plan of the North American continent – and finally the second British Two Year Plan in which six National Spiritual Assemblies worked together to establish the Faith on the continent of Africa. This Plan played a significant role in creating the pattern for future international cooperation and inter-Assembly projects – a prelude to the launching of world-encircling Plans throughout the planet.

Apart from these Plans, which had created an upsurge of activity among all the national Bahá'í communities and which had inspired many believers to arise as pioneers and settle in goal towns or in virgin territories, other important developments were taking place during this time paving the way for the future unfoldment and rise of the Administrative Order of Bahá'u'lláh. Foremost among these were the appointment by Shoghi Effendi in 1951 of the first contingent of the Hands of the Cause of God, whose number was soon to be increased, the formation in the same year of the International Bahá'í Council, destined to evolve through successive stages into the

Universal House of Justice, the participation of Bahá'í delegates in non-governmental organizations accredited to the United Nations and the phenomenal growth of the Faith in Africa, the first continent to witness entry into the Faith in great numbers.

These far-reaching achievements, together with the triumphant conclusion of all national Plans, endowed the community of the Most Great Name with tremendous potentialities for the expansion and consolidation of the Faith on a worldwide scale. The national communities had by then acquired the vision and capacity to take part in the first international Plan.

The Ten Year Crusade

Shoghi Effendi, in 1953, launched this Plan. Known as the Ten Year World Crusade, this historic Plan, referred to by the Guardian as the 'Greatest Spiritual Crusade'[33] the world has ever witnessed, marks at once the opening of the third and final phase of the initial epoch of the Tablets of the Divine Plan and the inception of the International Bahá'í Community, bringing together the 12 existing National Assemblies of the Bahá'í world for the purpose of implanting the banner of the Faith in all remaining virgin territories of the globe, multiplying the number of the Local and National Spiritual Assemblies throughout the world and accomplishing many other goals specified in the Plan.

At the time of the announcement of the goals of this mighty Crusade the followers of Bahá'u'lláh in every land were staggered by the immensity of the tasks with which they were confronted. Soon, however, they witnessed with feelings of gratitude, awe and wonder, that in the first year of the Plan alone one hundred virgin territories had been opened to the Faith![34]

This prodigious expansion of the Cause in the initial phase of the Plan, which inspired the army of Bahá'í pioneers and teachers to rise to loftier heights of heroism and sacrifice, enabling them to win further victories for the Cause and to accomplish all the major goals of the Plan in the following years, can only be attributed to the spirit of loyalty and devotion with which the Hands of the Cause of God and their Board members, the National and Local Assemblies, the pioneers and the teachers, one and all, turned to Shoghi Effendi, the Guardian of the Cause and the Sign of God on earth. It was halfway through this Plan, however, that the hand of God removed him suddenly from their midst and left the believers like orphans, grief-stricken and helpless, on their own.

Custodianship of the Hands of the Cause

Although Shoghi Effendi had passed away and, in his wisdom, had left no Will, the power of the Covenant played its part. The believers rallied around the Hands of the Cause of God, the 'Chief Stewards of Bahá'u'lláh's embryonic World Commonwealth'[35] who now assumed the function of guiding the Bahá'í world. This task they achieved by following strictly the guidance and the instructions of Shoghi Effendi outlined in his Ten Year Crusade. This period of about five years which stretches from the passing of Shoghi Effendi in 1957 until the election of the Universal House of Justice in 1963 can be considered as the most challenging phase in the history of the Formative Age of the Faith. This was a period in which the Covenant of Bahá'u'lláh was fully and rigorously tested and found to be absolutely impregnable. For, unlike the Universal House of Justice, the Hands of the Cause were not promised infallible guidance by Bahá'u'lláh. Yet, through their loyalty to Him and by their steadfastness in His Covenant, they guided the Bahá'í world exactly on the lines delineated by Shoghi Effendi in his writings and did not deviate one hair's breadth from the path shown by him.

Unlike the leaders of former religions who introduced so many man-made ideas into the teachings of their Prophets, the Hands of the Cause, in this period of their custodianship of the Faith of Bahá'u'lláh, did not add even a dot of their own to the Cause, nor did they introduce any innovations into the working of its institutions. Not only did they guide and assist the believers during this period of the Crusade, which was brought to its triumphant conclusion by them in 1963 when the Bahá'í community demonstrated, on the occasion of the Jubilee Celebration of the Declaration of

Bahá'u'lláh, its universality and cohesive strength but, at the same time, they handed over the Cause of God, pure and unadulterated, to the elected body of the Universal House of Justice upon whom Bahá'u'lláh has conferred infallibility and divine guidance.

At this juncture the Faith had grown from being merely a few national communities in 1952 into what was now a vast international community scattered throughout the world, with masses of people responding to the call of Bahá'u'lláh, recognizing His station and entering the Cause in great numbers. The number of countries, territories and islands opened to the Faith up to 1952 was 128; in 1963 it stood at 259. In 1952 there were just over 600 Local Spiritual Assemblies; this number was raised to over 3,400. In 1953 there were 12 National Spiritual Assemblies in existence: in 1962, 56 National and Regional Assemblies, whose members were the electors of the Universal House of Justice, came into being. The number of localities in which Bahá'ís resided throughout the world rose from about 2,400 to over 11,000 and the number of languages into which Bahá'í literature was translated increased from 89 to over 300. In many cases the progress of the Faith far exceeded the original goals set under the Plan. It was during this period also that three Mashriqu'l-Adhkárs (Houses of Worship) were built in the African, Australian and European continents, 46 additional sites were acquired for future Houses of Worship and 49 additional Ḥaẓíratu'l-Quds were obtained throughout the world.

Developments at the World Centre

In the Holy Land the process of building the World Centre of the Faith, which originated from Bahá'u'lláh through the revelation of the Tablet of Carmel and which was initiated by the hand of the Centre of His Covenant through the building of the original Mausoleum of the Báb, had, during the ministry of Shoghi Effendi, gathered such momentum that towards the end of his earthly life the glory of Carmel, foretold by the Prophets of the past, became manifest. The superstructure of the Shrine of the Báb, 'the Queen of Carmel', 'crowned in glowing gold, robed in shimmering white, girdled in emerald green' which enchanted 'every eye from air, sea, plain, and hill'[36] had been majestically raised. In its vicinity the monuments marking the resting places of the Greatest Holy Leaf, the Purest Branch and the mother and wife of 'Abdu'l-Bahá respectively, the focal point of a series of buildings, situated around an arc, which today constitute the international Administrative Centre of the Faith, had been befittingly erected. The first in this series – the International Archives Building – within whose walls the most precious relics of the Central Figures of the Faith are preserved, had been constructed. Nine terraces connecting the city of Haifa to the Shrine of the Báb had been completed and the gardens surrounding the Shrine and the adjoining buildings had been developed and embellished. The international endowments of the Faith stretching from the base of Mount Carmel to its summit, an area of over 350,000 square metres, had been acquired. A plot of land comprising approximately 36,000 square metres, for the purpose of erecting a Mashriqu'l-Adhkár on Mount Carmel located in 'close proximity to the Spot hallowed by the footsteps of Bahá'u'lláh, near the time-honoured Cave of Elijah, and associated with the revelation of the Tablet of Carmel, the Charter of the World Spiritual and Administrative Centres of the Faith on that mountain',[37] had finally, after tedious and prolonged negotiations, been purchased.

At Bahjí, the holiest spot in the Bahá'í world, around the Shrine of Bahá'u'lláh, within an area of approximately 160,000 square metres, beautiful gardens had been laid out and within these gardens where, in the future, a magnificent mausoleum over the Shrine of Bahá'u'lláh would be constructed, an outer sanctuary (termed the Ḥaram-i-Aqdas), designed to embrace this holy edifice, had been created. The realization of such magnificent achievements in the Holy Land during the opening years of the Formative Age of the Faith, together with the detailed delineation of the blueprint for the building of the World Centre of the Faith, setting the pattern for its future development, will always be regarded as one of the noblest fruits associated with the ministry of Shoghi Effendi.

The Universal House of Justice

The triumphant conclusion of the Ten Year Crusade, together with the termination of the interim period of the Custodianship of the Hands of the Cause marks, on the one hand, the closing of an epoch in the Formative Age and, on the other, the opening of a new one with the birth of the Universal House of Justice. An institution divinely ordained, infallibly guided by Bahá'u'lláh and the Báb, whose establishment had been anticipated by the Ancient Beauty in the Tablet of Carmel as the sailing of the 'Ark of God'[38] and whose functions have been clearly defined by Him in several Tablets, the Universal House of Justice has been described by the Master as the 'source of all good and freed from error'[39] and referred to by the Guardian as the 'apex of the Bahá'í Administrative Order',[40] the 'supreme organ of the Bahá'í Commonwealth'[41] and the 'last refuge of a tottering civilization'.[42]

In language most emphatic and clear 'Abdu'l-Bahá has, in the following passage, confirmed the authority of the Universal House of Justice:

> Unto the Most Holy Book every one must turn and all that is not expressly recorded therein must be referred to the Universal House of Justice. That which this body, whether unanimously or by a majority doth carry, that is verily the Truth and the Purpose of God himself. Whoso doth deviate therefrom is verily of them that love discord, hath shown forth malice, and turned away from the Lord of the Covenant.'[43]

And again: 'All must seek guidance and turn unto the Centre of the Cause and the House of Justice. And he that turneth unto whatsoever else is indeed in grievous error.'[44]

With the establishment of the Universal House of Justice the last and crowning edifice in the structure of the Administrative Order of Bahá'u'lláh had come into being and the outpouring of divine guidance had been restored. As we survey the history of the Faith from the time of the passing of Shoghi Effendi up to the birth of the Universal House of Justice, a period fraught with many dangers and uncertainties, we can clearly see that only through the power of the Covenant had the Bahá'í community preserved its unity and solidarity. Although scattered throughout the world and having different backgrounds, customs and languages, the mass of the believers remained steadfast in the Covenant and turned to the Centre of the Cause of God, the Universal House of Justice. Indeed, all that is contained within the Will and Testaments of Bahá'u'lláh and 'Abdu'l-Bahá, as far as the individual believer is concerned, can be condensed into one 'key word' and upon this word depends not only the spiritual life and the salvation of the individual but also the unity of the Bahá'í community. This word is to 'turn'. Bahá'u'lláh enjoined upon His followers to 'turn' to 'Abdu'l-Bahá after His ascension. 'Abdu'l-Bahá did likewise by directing them to 'turn' to Shoghi Effendi and the Universal House of Justice.

With a devotion and loyalty reminiscent of the early days of the Guardianship when steadfast Bahá'ís rallied around Shoghi Effendi, the believers all over the world 'turned' in this day to the Universal House of Justice. The wonderful messages of that august body which began, soon after its formation, to pour out from the World Centre, inspired the whole Bahá'í world and evoked feelings of joy and gratitude in the hearts of the believers who were then witnessing the power, the authority and the unerring guidance with which that supreme institution was fully invested.

The International Teaching Centre

This exalted institution was established in June 1973. In a cable dated 5 June 1973 to the Bahá'í world, the Universal House of Justice described the institution as

> DESTINED EVOLVE INTO ONE THOSE WORLD-SHAKING WORLD-EMBRACING WORLD-DIRECTING ADMINISTRATIVE INSTITUTIONS ORDAINED BY BAHÁ'U'LLÁH ANTICIPATED BY 'ABDU'L-BAHÁ ELUCIDATED BY SHOGHI EFFENDI.[45]

The following is a part of a letter written by the Universal House of Justice dated 8 June 1973 outlining the duties of the International Teaching Centre:

> The centennial year of the revelation of the Kitáb-i-Aqdas has already witnessed events of such capital significance in the annals of the Bahá'í Dispensation as to cause us to contemplate with awe the rapidity with which Divine Providence is advancing the Cause of the Most Great Name. The time is indeed propitious for the establishment of the International Teaching Centre, a development which, at one and the same time, brings to fruition the work of the Hands of the Cause residing in the Holy Land and provides for its extension into the future, links the institution of the Boards of Counsellors even more intimately with that of the Hands of the Cause of God, and powerfully reinforces the discharge of the rapidly growing responsibilities of the Universal House of Justice.
>
> This International Teaching Centre now established will, in due course, operate from that building designated by the Guardian as the Seat for the Hands of the Cause, which must be raised on the Arc on Mount Carmel in close proximity to the Seat of the Universal House of Justice.
>
> The duties now assigned to this nascent institution are:
>
> - To coordinate, stimulate and direct the activities of the Continental Boards of Counsellors and to act as liaison between them and the Universal House of Justice.
> - To be fully informed of the situation of the Cause in all parts of the world and to be able, from the background of this knowledge, to make reports and recommendations to the Universal House of Justice and the Continental Boards of Counsellors.
> - To be alert to possibilities, both within and without the Bahá'í community, for the extension of the teaching work into receptive or needy areas, and to draw

the attention of the Universal House of Justice and the Continental Boards of Counsellors to such possibilities, making recommendations for action.

- To determine and anticipate needs for literature, pioneers and travelling teachers and to work out teaching plans, both regional and global, for the approval of the Universal House of Justice.

All the Hands of the Cause of God will be members of the International Teaching Centre. Each Hand will be kept regularly informed of the activities of the Centre through reports or copies of its minutes, and will be able, wherever he may be residing or travelling, to convey suggestions, recommendations and information to the Centre and, whenever he is in the Holy Land, to take part in the consultations and other activities of the Centre . . .

At present three Hands of the Cause of God Amatu'l-Bahá Ruḥíyyih Khánum, Mr Furútan and Dr Varqá and nine Counsellors constitute the membership of this lofty institution.

The Nine Year Plan

The Universal House of Justice, in 1964, launched a Nine Year world-embracing Plan which was to be a forerunner of a series of Plans extending over 'successive epochs of both the Formative and the Golden Ages of the Faith'.[46] It ushered in the second epoch of the Tablets of the Divine Plan and called for the expansion of the Faith and the establishment of its institutions on a much vaster scale than ever before. Among other things, it aimed to increase, by the end of the Plan in 1973, the number of localities in which Bahá'ís resided to over 54,000, the number of National Spiritual Assemblies to 114 and the number of Local Spiritual Assemblies to almost 14,000.[47]

With a zeal and enthusiasm no less ardent and soul-stirring and a determination no less unyielding than that which inspired the Bahá'ís of an earlier epoch of the Formative Age, thousands of believers, from all over the world, arose for the accomplishment of the goals of this world-embracing Plan. Through sacrificial efforts and by pioneering and teaching, they won memorable victories for the Cause of God. The process of 'entry by troops' into the Faith of God foretold by 'Abdu'l-Bahá continued with ever-increasing momentum in some parts of the world. The significant messages of Bahá'u'lláh addressed to the kings and rulers of the world in His day, summoning them to recognize His station and embrace His Cause were, in a fitting manner, presented to the great majority of the heads of state throughout the globe. The process of the proclamation of His message to the generality of mankind, paving the way for the complete emergence of the Faith of God from obscurity and leading to its emancipation from the fetters of religious orthodoxy and its recognition as an independent religion, had accelerated.

By the end of the Plan, great strides had been made at the World Centre of the Faith towards the implementation of many important goals, including the codification of the Kitáb-i-Aqdas, the formulation of the Constitution of the Universal House of Justice, the extension into the future of the Hands' functions of protection and propagation through the appointment of several Boards of Counsellors, the collation and classification of the writings of Bahá'u'lláh, 'Abdu'l-Bahá and Shoghi Effendi, the extension of the Bahá'í properties in the Holy Land and the development and beautification of the gardens surrounding the holy Shrines.

The aim and purpose of this Plan, and others which followed, was to diffuse the light of the Faith of Bahá'u'lláh throughout the world and to build up a new World Order for the whole of mankind. This new World Order is now, like an embryo, growing amidst the tumult and chaos of a decaying order which is swiftly heading towards its doom and destruction.

The Analogy of the Old House and the New House

The old order can be likened to an old house inside whose walls mankind for centuries has been sheltered and within whose many parts nations of the world have lived in comparative isolation until the coming of Bahá'u'lláh when a new life was breathed into all created things and a new era dawned upon humanity. In His Tablets Bahá'u'lláh, in unmistakable terms, proclaimed to the peoples of the world: 'Soon will the present-day order be rolled up, and a new one spread out in its stead.'[48] He warned them that the old house was no longer going to provide a safe shelter for mankind and that before long it would fall apart. He called on the peoples of the world to come out of the old house and, under His guidance, begin the building of a new one. This clarion call of Bahá'u'lláh fell on deaf ears. Only a handful from among His own countrymen at first recognized Him as the redeemer of mankind and the architect of a new house, this new World Order. These left the old house and came out to prepare the way for the building of a new one.

The first and most important part of any building is the laying of its foundations and the initial step here is that of excavation. This is a stage in which everything is being pulled down instead of raised up and the work does not seem to be constructive. In the early days of the Faith, therefore, the outside world failed to appreciate the glorious work performed by a small band of heroic souls who laboured with matchless heroism and self-sacrifice in order to prepare the way for the building of a new house – this world-encircling Order. This was a period of persecution and martyrdom, a period during which, in the terms of our analogy, storms of dust were raised by the process of excavating the foundations of the new house and humanity as a whole looked upon it as a useless operation. Indeed, the stories of heroism and martyrdom reached the people of the East and the West and yet, the generality of mankind – the inhabitants of the old house – busied with their own affairs and deprived of spiritual vision, saw nothing of the glory and greatness of those 77 years which marked the duration of the Heroic Age and prepared the way for the laying of the foundations of the new World Order of Bahá'u'lláh in a later period.

With the advent of the Formative Age in 1921, the time for the actual building of the new house had at last come. The Bahá'ís of the world, under the guidance of Shoghi Effendi, their beloved Guardian, had begun the task of laying its foundations. After 50 years of dedicated service, of toil and labour on the part of the builders of Bahá'u'lláh's World Order, the form and pattern of the new house which is destined to shelter, in the fullness of time, the whole of the human race within its walls, is gradually emerging from the ruins of the old order, attracting to itself each day, in ever-increasing numbers, men and women from all walks of life who have been disenchanted with the old house.

The others, who constitute the majority of mankind, are, alas, in the words of Bahá'u'lláh, 'bereft of discernment to see God with their own eyes, or hear His Melody with their own ears'.[49] Fettered by age-long traditions and bound within the clutches of an ailing order, the inhabitants of the old house have their vision obscured by many veils which are placed before their eyes. Such veils as materialism and prejudice, pride and vainglory, prevent them from seeing the grandeur and the beauty of the new house majestically rising amidst the chaos of a divided world.

Today the forces of destruction are sweeping the face of the earth and the old house is increasingly being shaken to its very foundations. Within it, mankind, agonized and confused, is struggling hopelessly to mend a structure which is rapidly disintegrating and which is completely beyond repair.

'The world is in travail,' wrote Bahá'u'lláh almost one hundred years ago,

> and its agitation waxeth day by day. Its face is turned towards waywardness and unbelief. Such shall be its plight, that to disclose it now would not be meet and seemly. Its perversity will long continue. And when the appointed hour is come, there shall suddenly appear that which shall cause the limbs of mankind to quake. Then, and only then, will the Divine Standard be unfurled, and the Nightingale of Paradise warble its melody.[50]

The followers of Bahá'u'lláh, having realized that the old house is not repairable and that it will eventually fall apart, labour in every land with the utmost dedication and a sense of extreme urgency in the building of the new house. Although anxious to give a helping hand to the unfortunate and the down-trodden and eager to alleviate the misery and suffering of their fellow men in the old house, Bahá'ís are nevertheless conscious that the old order is doomed to failure and that such assistance will be only of a very limited value and will not, in the end, solve the problems of mankind. They clearly see that when the world is suffering from so many ills their only task is the revivification of its peoples and the complete reorientation of human society.

Bahá'ís remain loyal to their respective governments and do not participate in partisan politics. Only in this way can they remain faithful to the mission entrusted to them by Bahá'u'lláh, a mission which is to build, in the Formative Age, a new World Order for mankind.

The First Half-century of the Formative Age

Great indeed is the spectacle that appears before us as we survey the momentous events of the first half-century of the Formative Age of the Faith – an Age which witnessed, on the eve of the passing of the Master, the birth of the Administrative Order of Bahá'u'lláh. A cursory review of the history of the Cause will demonstrate that a Faith that had been oppressed in the land of its birth from its very inception, had sustained a most grievous blow in the martyrdom of its Herald, had suffered the unbearable tribulations heaped upon its Author, had witnessed the martyrdom of no less than 20,000 of its adherents and which was, as anticipated by Náṣiri'd-Dín Sháh, its royal adversary, to have its very name obliterated from the pages of history, has acquired during the first 50 years of the Formative Age such vitality and strength and made such phenomenal progress as to astonish its own avowed adherents as well as its enemies.

The light of the Faith that was ignited in the Síyáh-Chál of Ṭihrán, whose brilliance was fully manifested in Adrianople, whose rays illumined parts of the American, the European and the Australian continents during the ministry of the Master has, during the early period of the Formative Age, systematically been diffused to almost 50,000 localities in the world. The 'Army of Light' consisting of pioneers, teachers and administrators recruited from every race, class and colour, proclaiming to mankind the advent of the Lord of Hosts, has encircled the globe. The Faith of Bahá'u'lláh has reached almost every stratum of human society. Its fundamental verities, its history, its teachings, its transforming power and its aim and purpose, have been, and are being, increasingly brought to the attention of a tormented humanity. The rising institutions of its divinely guided Administrative Order have been established; and within its World Centre, in the vicinity of its holy Shrines, the crowning edifice of that same Order – the Universal House of Justice which will, in the fullness of time, unveil to mankind its glorious station and manifest the sovereignty of Bahá'u'lláh – has been majestically erected.

The winning of such memorable victories for the Cause within so short a period of time, foreshadowing the advent of much greater achievements in the future, is due primarily to the rise of the Administrative Order whose significance Shoghi Effendi has extolled in these words:

> Let no one, while this System is still in its infancy, misconceive its character, belittle its significance or misrepresent its purpose. The bedrock on which this Administrative Order is founded is God's immutable Purpose for mankind in this day. The Source from which it derives its inspiration is no one less than Bahá'u'lláh Himself. Its shield and defender are the embattled hosts of the Abhá Kingdom. Its seed is the blood of no less than twenty thousand martyrs who have offered up their lives that it may be born and flourish. The axis round which its institutions revolve are the authentic provisions of the Will and Testament of 'Abdu'l-Bahá. Its guiding principles are the truths which He Who is the unerring Interpreter of the teachings of our Faith has so clearly enunciated in His public addresses throughout the West. The laws that govern

> its operation and limit its functions are those which have been expressly ordained in the Kitáb-i-Aqdas. The seat round which its spiritual, its humanitarian and administrative activities will cluster are the Mashriqu'l-Adhkár and its Dependencies. The pillars that sustain its authority and buttress its structure are the twin institutions of the Guardianship and of the Universal House of Justice. The central, the underlying aim which animates it is the establishment of the New World Order as adumbrated by Bahá'u'lláh. The methods it employs, the standard it inculcates, incline it to neither East nor West, neither Jew nor Gentile, neither rich nor poor, neither white nor coloured. Its watchword is the unification of the human race; its standard the 'Most Great Peace'; its consummation the advent of that golden millennium – the Day when the kingdoms of this world shall have become the Kingdom of God Himself, the Kingdom of Bahá'u'lláh.[51]

Other Major Developments During and Since the Nine Year Plan

Since the publication of the first edition of this book in 1972 and subsequent to the completion of the Nine Year Plan, a series of international teaching plans have been launched and successfully implemented throughout the Bahá'í world: the Five Year Plan (1974–9), the Seven Year Plan (1979– 86), the Six Year Plan (1986–92), the Three Year Plan (1993–6) and the Four Year Plan (1996–2000). In 2000 the Universal House of Justice focused the Bahá'í world on a series of Plans which, it indicated, will take the community to 2021.

> The two stages in the unfoldment of the Divine Plan lying immediately ahead will last one year and five years respectively. At Riḍván 2000 the Bahá'í world will be asked to embark on the first of these two stages, a twelve-month effort aimed at concentrating the forces, the capacities and the insights that have so strongly emerged. The Five Year Plan that follows will initiate a series of worldwide enterprises that will carry the

> Bahá'í community through the final twenty years in the first century of the Faith's Formative Age. These global Plans will continue to focus on advancing the process of entry by troops and on its systematic acceleration.[52]

From its very inception, the Cause of God has gone through severe persecutions perpetrated by its enemies; Shoghi Effendi explains this phenomenon in these words:

> . . . with every fresh outbreak of hostility to the Faith, whether from within or from without, a corresponding measure of outpouring grace, sustaining its defenders and confounding its adversaries, has been providentially released, communicating a fresh impulse to the onward march of the Faith, while this impetus, in its turn, would through its manifestations, provoke fresh hostility in quarters heretofore unaware of its challenging implications . . .
>
> The resistless march of the Faith of Bahá'u'lláh, viewed in this light, and propelled by the stimulating influences which the unwisdom of its enemies and the force latent within itself both engender, resolves itself into a series of rhythmic pulsations, precipitated, on the one hand, through the explosive outbursts of its foes, and the vibrations of Divine Power, on the other, which speed it, with ever-increasing momentum, along that predestined course traced for it by the Hand of the Almighty.[53]

Never before have these twin processes of crisis and victory been so clearly demonstrated as in this period when the Bahá'ís of Iran are being persecuted by the enemies of the Faith. Fierce persecution of the Bahá'ís of Iran began in 1979 and continues to the present time, resulting in the martyrdom of over 200 believers. This includes the confiscation of all Bahá'í holy places and endowments; the disbanding of all Bahá'í administrative institutions; the demolition of the House of the Báb, the sacred place of pilgrimage; the demolition of the House of Bahá'u'lláh in Ṭihrán; the denial of higher education to Bahá'í youth; and the withholding of basic human rights from the Bahá'ís, resulting in expressions of support for the Bahá'ís by governments and the peoples of the world and a global condemnation of the persecution of the Bahá'ís in Iran.

Listed below are some of the major developments in the Bahá'í world from 1972 to 2008. The author made a list of developments from 1972 to 1999. This was brought up to date in 2008. For ease of access this list has been broadly categorized.

Developments at the World Centre

- Acquisition in 1973 of the Mansion of Mazra'ih, the residence of Bahá'u'lláh after His departure from the city of 'Akká; the restoration of the building and extension of the gardens surrounding it.
- Acquisition in 1975 and restoration of the House of 'Abdu'lláh Pá<u>sh</u>á, which served as 'Abdu'l-Bahá's residence in 'Akká for several years.
- Completion of the Seat of the Universal House of Justice on Mount Carmel and its occupation in 1983. From this majestic building, the world-vitalizing forces of guidance and enlightenment stream forth to the Bahá'í world.
- Celebration in January 2001 of the occupation by the International Teaching Centre of its permanent seat on Mount Carmel, one of the 'historic happenings of the Formative Age'[54] attended by Counsellors and Auxiliary Board members from around the world.
- Holding of a major event in May 2001 at the World Centre attended by representatives of all Bahá'í communities throughout the world to mark the completion of the projects on Mount Carmel, bringing into being 'a vastly augmented World Centre structure which will be capable of meeting the challenges of coming centuries and of the tremendous growth of the Bahá'í community . . .'[55] These projects comprised the creation of 18

terraces ranged above and below the Shrine of the Báb; the construction of the Centre for the Study of the Sacred Texts and the Seat of the International Teaching Centre; and the extension of the basement of the Archives building.

- Further extension and beautification of gardens and lands associated with the Holy Places in the twin cities of 'Akká and Haifa and their surrounding areas
- A significant increase in the numbers of pilgrims, made possible by the creation of new facilities for their reception.

Application of the Laws of Bahá'u'lláh

- Introduction of the law of Ḥuqúqu'lláh to the West in 1984 and its worldwide application in 1992. Under the guiding hand of Trustee of Ḥuqúqu'lláh Hand of the Cause of God 'Alí-Muḥammad Varqá, this was followed by the establishment of Boards of Trustees throughout the world, culminating in 2005 with the establishment of the International Board of Trustees.
- The universal application in 1999 of all of the elements of the laws dealing with obligatory prayer and fasting, as well as the daily repetition of Alláh-u-Abhá 95 times.

Significant Global Developments

- Persecution of the Bahá'ís in Iran, Egypt and other countries.
- Announcements by the Universal House of Justice that the Formative Age had entered into its fourth epoch in 1986 and its fifth epoch in 2001.
- Completion of the Houses of Worship in Panama City, Panama; Apia, Western Samoa; and New Delhi, India; and announcement of plans for the construction of a House of Worship in Santiago, Chile.
- Acceptance of the Faith by His Highness Malietoa

Tanumafili II, the King of Western Samoa, in 1973.

- Designation by the Universal House of Justice of the period between 21 April 1992 and 20 April 1993 as a Holy Year in tribute to Bahá'u'lláh and in honour of the hundredth anniversary of His Ascension.
- Commemoration of the hundredth anniversary of the Ascension of Bahá'u'lláh held in the precincts of the Shrine of Bahá'u'lláh at Bahjí, attended by the Knights of Bahá'u'lláh and nearly three thousand believers, representing every national community throughout the world.
- Convocation in November 1992 of the second Bahá'í World Congress, in New York, the City of the Covenant, attended by about 27,000 followers of Bahá'u'lláh from every background and representing all strata of human society, celebrating in a jubilant spirit the hundredth anniversary of the inauguration of the Covenant of Bahá'u'lláh; and the simultaneous convocation of nine regional conferences on five continents linked to the World Congress by satellite transmission.
- Holding of eight international conferences in 1976–7, five in 1982 and 41 in 2008–9.

Emergence from Obscurity and the Entrance of the Cause onto the World Scene

- Emergence of the Faith from obscurity and its growing recognition by world leaders and governments, who, in some instances, have sought Bahá'í views on and solutions to various social and moral problems facing humanity today.
- The advancement of the international Bahá'í community in the field of external affairs aimed at promoting the processes of world peace, particularly through involvement of the community in the fields of moral education, global prosperity, the status of women and human rights.

- Establishment of the Office of Public Information at the World Centre with its auxiliary agencies in New York and other parts of the world.
- Establishment of Bahá'í Chairs at universities, including in 1993 the Bahá'í Chair for World Peace at the University of Maryland, USA; a Chair for Bahá'í Studies at the University of Indore, India; and the Chair for Bahá'í Studies at the Hebrew University of Jerusalem in 1999.
- Considerable expansion of the role on the world stage of the Bahá'í International Community, granted consultative status with the UN Economic and Social Council in 1970 and with the United Nations Fund for Children (UNICEF) in 1976; and the establishment in New York of the Office for the Environment in 1989 and of the Office for the Advancement of Women in 1992.
- Appointment in 2000 of the Bahá'í International Community representative as co-chair of the NGO Millennium Forum and his addressing the Millennium Summit on behalf of the NGO community.
- Establishment of the Office of Social and Economic Development at the Bahá'í World Centre in 1983 and the subsequent incorporation of social and economic development activities in the regular pursuits of the worldwide Bahá'í community.

Growth of the Faith and Efforts to Advance the Process of Entry by Troops

- Commencement in 1996 of a Four Year Plan which had one major aim, which is to continue until the year 2021: a significant advance in the process of entry by troops. By the year 2000 a 'marked progress in the activity and development of the individual believer, of the institutions, and of the local community'[56] was being achieved through the establishment of a system of training institutes throughout the world.

- Emergence of a new culture of growth in the Bahá'í world community towards the end of the 20th century and the early years of the 21st. National communities mapped their territories into geographic clusters and within these concentrated attention on two movements: a steady flow of believers through a sequence of courses offered by training institutes and the movement of clusters through stages of growth. Administrative agencies evolved at a cluster level to support these two movements and the teaching work.
- Efficacy of the training provided by the institutes enabled hundreds of thousands of believers to acquire the knowledge, spiritual insights and skills and attributes required to carry out acts of service that would sustain large scale expansion and consolidation. Among these acts of service are four core activities which are open to the wider community:
  - study circles, through contact with the Word of God provide the training described above
  - devotional gatherings
  - junior youth programmes, designed to inculcate a spirit of service to humanity
  - children's classes, for the spiritual and moral education of children
- Setting of a goal for 1,500 clusters worldwide to establish intensive programmes of growth for the Five Year Plan commencing at Riḍván 2006.
- By the year 2008 systematic action and a culture of learning – a process of action, consultation, reflection and planning – characterized the manner in which the community functioned. This coherent approach is gradually being applied to other areas of the work of the Faith.

- Considerable expansion of the Faith in all republics of the former Soviet Union and countries of Eastern Europe and the establishment of Local and National Spiritual Assemblies.
- Worldwide cooperation among various National Spiritual Assemblies resulting in the implementation of numerous inter-assembly projects as set out in the various teaching plans.
- Youth in the forefront of all aspects of the work of the Cause.
- Establishment of the Youth Year of Service.

Development of the Institutions of the Faith

- The passing of Amatu'l-Bahá Rúḥíyyih Khánum, wife of the Guardian, and the other remaining Hands of the Cause of God brought to an end 'the remarkable stewardship of an institution whose legacy is unparalleled in religious history!' [57]
- Appointment in 1973 of the International Teaching Centre and the introduction of assistants to the Auxiliary Board members in the same year. The number of Continental Counsellors stood at 72 and Auxiliary Board members at one thousand in 2008.
- Local and National Spiritual Assemblies have been strengthened and their number increased. In April 2008 there were 184 National Spiritual Assemblies functioning throughout the world.
- The establishment, in selected countries where conditions necessitated their formation, of Regional Bahá'í Councils with autonomous decision-making powers for both teaching and administrative matters.
- Marked increase in the effectiveness of the collaboration between the Institution of the Counsellors and National and Local Spiritual Assemblies and their agencies.

Literature

- Publication of the first edition of the English translation of the Kitáb-i-Aqdas, the Mother Book of this Dispensation, complete with supplementary materials and numerous annotations, and its subsequent translation into other languages.
- Publication of authorized English translations of scripture: *The Tablets of Bahá'u'lláh Revealed after the Kitáb-i-Aqdas*, *The Summons of the Lord of Hosts*, The Long Healing Prayer, The Fire Tablet, *Gems of Divine Mysteries*, *The Tabernacle of Unity*, *Selections from the Writings of the Báb* and *Selections from the Writings of 'Abdu'l-Bahá*.
- Publication of several thematic compilations of the writings of Bahá'u'lláh, 'Abdu'l-Bahá, Shoghi Effendi and letters of the Universal House of Justice.
- The preparation of a new translation of *Some Answered Questions*.
- Continued collation and classification of the sacred texts.
- Considerable increase in the publication of Bahá'í literature in various languages.

Major Statements and Other Important Documents

- Dissemination of 'The Promise of World Peace', a letter addressed by the Universal House of Justice to the peoples of the world outlining the progress made towards peace and the remaining obstacles to it, and its presentation to heads of state and other world leaders as well as to the general public in most countries.
- Dissemination of the April 2002 letter of the Universal House of Justice addressed to 'The World's Religious Leaders, which 'calls on religious leadership for a break with the past as decisive as those that opened the way

for society to address equally corrosive prejudices of race, gender and nation'.[58]

- Commissioning of *Century of Light,* a document addressing the relationship between the profound changes that took place in the world and within the Bahá'í community during the 20th century.
- Production of numerous statements on issues of world concern by the Bahá'í International Community including *Bahá'u'lláh*, *The Prosperity of Humankind*, *Turning Point for All Nations* and *Who is Writing the Future?*
- Bestowal by the UN Secretary-General of the title 'Peace Messenger' on the Bahá'í International Community and five National Spiritual Assemblies – Australia, Belgium, Brazil, Kenya and Lesotho – an honour given to only 300 organizations worldwide

THE SPIRITUAL DEVELOPMENT OF THE INDIVIDUAL

The Revelation of Bahá'u'lláh confers upon the individual believer the gift of faith, and as one draws closer to Bahá'u'lláh, one's soul will grow in spirituality and attain greater enlightenment in the realms of the spirit. In order to appreciate this phenomenon, it is necessary to understand the powers and qualities of the human soul. A study of the writings of Bahá'u'lláh and 'Abdu'l-Bahá on this subject reveals that the soul does not originate from the world of matter; it is an emanation from the spiritual worlds of God. During the period when the embryo is growing in the womb of the mother, the soul becomes associated with the body. Because the soul is a spiritual and not a material entity, it does not enter the body or leave it. The soul is exalted above entry or exit, ascent or descent. It is independent of any earthly agency. Its association with the body is similar to the association of light with a mirror. The light is not inside the mirror; it is reflected in it and when the mirror is removed, the light remains unaffected.

Since the soul is exalted above all physical creation, our minds are incapable of grasping its nature and powerless to fathom its essence. We can perceive only the attributes and qualities of the soul. In this life we have a limited capacity to understand spiritual verities. Our knowledge of the soul is derived from the Manifestations of God who, through their words, have conveyed some of its significance. Words are inadequate tools for explaining spiritual realities.

A study of the writings of Bahá'u'lláh makes it clear that God's creation is one entity. It includes both the spiritual and physical worlds. The same laws and principles in nature are to be found in the spiritual realms but they are applied on a higher level and contain features non-existent in the lower kingdom.

Physical and Spiritual Counterparts

Because the basic principles and laws of existence run through the whole of creation, many of the physical phenomena we notice on this earth have counterparts in the spiritual realms. Let us therefore examine some aspects of the soul in the light of these common principles. From a study of the writings of Bahá'u'lláh and 'Abdu'l-Bahá it appears that the counterpart of the soul in this physical world is the embryo growing in the womb. We note many similarities between the two and the knowledge of the one will lead to a limited understanding of the other.

We know that a child's physical body grows in the womb of the mother and acquires limbs and organs which are only needed after birth. The same principle applies to the soul. For the soul progresses in the womb of this world acquiring spiritual qualities which are essential to its existence in the next life. The child in the womb of the mother and the soul in this life are indeed counterparts.

The Soul Acquires Good Qualities

We notice in the physical world that the embryo in the womb of the mother starts life with one cell. With the passage of time the cell multiplies, limbs and organs come into existence, eventually the embryonic life comes to an end and the child is born as a perfect being. Here we see the vast contrast between the first cell at the beginning and its consumation at the time of birth.

The same phenomenon occurs with the soul. At its inception it is without experience and its qualities and powers lie latent within it. As a result of its association with the body in this womb-world, its individuality develops and it later acquires spiritual qualities and divine attributes which it carries to the next world. But the soul cannot take with it bad qualities, for in fact these do not exist and are but the lack of good qualities, just as poverty does not have an existence of its own and is the lack of riches. If a man has lived an ungodly life, his soul is impoverished and can take only a small measure of goodness with it to the next world.

From a study of the writings we gather that, similar to this world where there are degrees of existence, such as the mineral, the vegetable, the animal and the human – and even in each kingdom there are divisions – in the spiritual worlds of God the human soul will also progress on different levels depending on what good qualities a soul takes with it to the next world. Those on the lower level will not be able to understand those on the higher one. Here we see an example of how the same principle that operates in the physical world, namely the diversity of God's creation, is also operative in the spiritual realms.

Where is the Next World?

Another example is the principle that higher forms of life revolve around and depend upon the lowest. In this physical world we observe that all living things derive their sustenance from the mineral world which is the lowest kingdom. In one of His Tablets Bahá'u'lláh testifies that all the spiritual worlds revolve around this world. This indicates that the next world is not divorced from life in this world but rather encompasses it. We see in nature that the child grows in the womb of the mother, unable to discover that the world into which it is destined to be born is amazingly close to it. Only a thin barrier separates the two worlds. Again this principle applies in the spiritual realms. The soul will discover after its separation from the body how close the spiritual world has been to it. But as long as it is in this mortal abode, the next world and its grandeur are hidden from its eyes.

Bahá'u'lláh states in one of His Tablets that should the station destined for a true believer in the world beyond be revealed to the extent of a needle's eye, every soul would expire in ecstasy! Just as the unborn child is incapable of discovering the vastness and beauty of this world, so the soul cannot discern the exalted domain of the spiritual world while on this earth.

The Main Purpose of Creation

What then is the purpose of creation in light of Bahá'u'lláh's Revelation? 'The purpose of God in creating man', Bahá'u'lláh proclaims, 'hath been, and will ever be, to enable him to know his Creator and to attain His Presence.'[59] And this can be attained through the recognition of His Manifestation. By turning to Him and receiving the outpourings of His glory, the soul gives birth to the spirit of faith. It is not unlike the birth of a child. The child cannot come into existence without a father, and the soul cannot acquire the spirit of faith without the assistance of the Manifestation of God. The soul needs to recognize and establish a spiritual link with Him.

By turning to Bahá'u'lláh with devotion, by learning to love Him, by submitting itself to the influence of His Revelation and by establishing spiritual communion with Him, the soul will become fertilized and will give birth to the spirit of faith. This is the ultimate and most glorious destiny for the soul, the purpose for which it was created.

Therefore, when the individual recognizes Bahá'u'lláh as the Manifestation of God in this age, the believer's soul becomes endowed with the spirit of faith. This is like a spark that is ignited in the heart. This spark is at first like a faint glimmer of light but it must be allowed to become a fire with an ever growing intensity. It is then that the believer will fall in love with Bahá'u'lláh. The question is how a person who has just embraced the Faith can draw closer to Bahá'u'lláh, to fan into flame the spark of his faith and increase the intensity of love for Him day by day.

It is stated in the Qur'án, and Bahá'u'lláh confirms and reiterates, that 'Knowledge is a light which God casteth into the heart of whomsoever He willeth'.[60] The statement that the heart is the dawning-place of the knowledge of God may sound strange to some, because it is known that the mind is the vehicle for acquiring knowledge and not the heart. But faith and knowledge of God, like seeds, are first planted in the heart. Subsequently the mind grasps the truth and begins to understand it. In the end it is the interaction of the two – the heart and the mind – that brings confirmation and certitude to the soul.

Intellectual Approach Not Sufficient

Although initially faith in Bahá'u'lláh may come to a believer through an intellectual approach, its intensification and growth day by day cannot continue purely by intellectual pursuits. And if a person's faith does not grow with the passage of time it is like a child who is born but has failed to grow. In such a case, the believer is very likely to feel a measure of doubt concerning the Faith and may experience great mental conflict when confronted with tests. Although intellectually the individual may accept Bahá'u'lláh as a Manifestation of God and may even be well versed in His writings, such a person will not be able to have that absolute certitude which endows a human being with spiritual qualities and confers upon one's soul perpetual contentment, assurance and happiness.

The heart is a focal point of warmth and love. The characteristic of the heart is to fall in love with another party, and it is the individual who finds and chooses that party. For example, if one turns one's affections to the material world, the heart will become attached to material things very easily. But if the individual turns to God and spiritual things, then one's heart can fall in love with Him provided that the person fulfils one condition stated by Bahá'u'lláh in these words: 'O Son of Being! Thy heart is My home; sanctify it for My descent.'[61] How do we sanctify the heart? Bahá'u'lláh in another passage explains:

> O Son of Dust! All that is in heaven and earth I have ordained for thee, except the human heart, which I have made the habitation of My beauty and glory; yet thou didst give My home and dwelling to another than Me; and whenever the manifestation of My holiness sought His own abode, a stranger found He there, and, homeless, hastened unto the sanctuary of the Beloved.[62]

and again

> O My Friend in Word! Ponder awhile. Hast thou ever heard that friend and foe should abide in one heart? Cast out then the stranger, that the Friend may enter His home.[63]

Therefore to acquire faith and enable the Revelation of God to shine within the heart, we must cast out the 'stranger'.

Who is This Stranger?

'The stranger' may be regarded as our attachment to this world, and the most formidable type of attachment, and the most harmful, is attachment to one's own self. Such self attachment manifests itself mainly in the form of pride in one's own knowledge and other accomplishments such as rank and position. It is the love of one's own self that renders the individual opinionated, self-centred, proud and egotistical. In fact, it denudes the individual of spiritual qualities. Such a person has indeed harboured within the heart a great enemy, namely, the 'stranger', and even upon acceptance of the Faith, that person will find it difficult to derive spiritual upliftment from the writings of Bahá'u'lláh because attachment to one's own self has become a barrier between the individual and God.

To read the writings with the eye of intellect, while proudly regarding oneself as a being endowed with great qualities and accomplishments, will undoubtedly close the door to the bounties and confirmations of Bahá'u'lláh and His words cannot influence the heart. Of course, when one recognizes Bahá'u'lláh as the Manifestation of God one becomes humble before Him and this is one of the main prerequisites for driving 'the stranger' step by step, out of one's heart. 'Humble thyself before Me, that I may graciously visit thee'[64] is Bahá'u'lláh's clear admonition to us.

> Blind thine eyes, that thou mayest behold My beauty; stop thine ears, that thou mayest hearken unto the sweet melody of My voice; empty thyself of all learning, that thou mayest

> partake of My knowledge; and sanctify thyself from riches, that thou mayest obtain a lasting share from the ocean of My eternal wealth.[65]

There is a beautiful Persian story in verse concerning a drop of rain falling from the clouds. The drop knows itself to be the water of life, the most precious element that God has created, so it is proud of itself. Boasting all the way down it suddenly sees an ocean beneath. It then recognizes its own insignificance and exclaims: 'If this exists, then what am I?' When the ocean hears this expression of humility it attracts the drop to itself and makes it a companion of the pearl.

The following is part of an obligatory prayer by Bahá'u'lláh. Though very brief, it is reminiscent of the story of the drop and the ocean and a perfect confession of who we are:

> I bear witness, O my God, that Thou hast created me to know Thee and to worship Thee. I testify, at this moment, to my powerlessness and to Thy might, to my poverty and to Thy wealth.[66]

When, through his own endeavours and with the help of prayer the individual succeeds in catching a glimpse of the majesty and grandeur of Bahá'u'lláh, just as for the drop when it saw the ocean, the soul will progress step by step until it becomes the embodiment of self-effacement and utter nothingness, which is the highest attainment for a human being and the essential characteristic of a spiritual giant.

Then and only then can the individual drive the 'stranger' away.

Spiritual Food

As we have already stated, when a person's heart is touched by the love of Bahá'u'lláh and says 'I believe', the spirit of faith is newly born in one's soul. This is the second birth spoken of in the Gospels. Like a new-born babe which has to take food in order to grow, we have to take spiritual food to nourish our souls.

The spiritual food is the word of God revealed by Bahá'u'lláh for this age. By reading His words, the spirit of faith will grow step by step and the believer will become steadfast in faith, and assured and happy in life. If one neglects this vital necessity, one's faith will diminish in strength and one may even lose it altogether.

The First Step Towards Spiritual Growth is Reading the Holy Writings

Like a mother who offers food to her child several times a day, Bahá'u'lláh has enjoined His followers to recite His words twice a day, in the morning and the evening, and states that those who do not recite them are not faithful to the Covenant of God.

Now let us study the significance of the commandment of Bahá'u'lláh to recite His words twice a day.

We know that in all His domains and kingdoms God communicates with His creation through some instrument. For example, the sun shedding its rays upon all physical creation is one of the means by which God communicates with all created things on this earth, releasing thereby such vivifying energies as are necessary for growth and development.

The means by which our Creator communicates with our souls, however, is through the instrumentality of the words revealed by the Manifestation of God, in this day Bahá'u'lláh. The very thought that our Creator, wishing to communicate with our souls, has chosen to 'talk' to us through the words of Bahá'u'lláh, and that, like the rays of the sun, His words illumine our beings, is sufficient to create such an excitement in our hearts as believers that we will take the book of God into our hands with feelings of joy and reverence, knowing as we read the words that our Creator is 'talking' to us, shedding His light upon our innermost heart and showering His bounties upon us. We can receive all these precious favours provided we succeed in driving the 'stranger' away and with a pure heart turn to God. Thus we can open the book of God with great confidence that through the potency of the words revealed therein we will be enabled to grow spiritually.

At this juncture it is useful to note the difference between saying prayers and reciting the writings. These two are sometimes opposite things. Often when we say a prayer we ask God for something but when we recite the Tablets and holy writings it is God who asks us to carry out His commandments.

In the Kitáb-i-Aqdas Bahá'u'lláh states that there is no merit in reading His words when tired. He says to read a few lines with a spirit of joy and fragrance is better than to read a whole book when depressed and weary. This commandment is very much in tune with the law of nature that a person eat food only when he is hungry. Another similarity is that in nature one must eat food regularly every day. To eat once in a lifetime is not sufficient. It is the same with reading the words of God which are the food for the spirit. To read the holy writings once in a while is not enough. As ordained by Bahá'u'lláh, the individual must, if the soul is to grow spiritually, read His words, which are recorded in His tablets, twice every day.

Allow the Power of the Words to Enter into Our Hearts

These words with all their vivifying forces must then be allowed to penetrate into the heart and to strengthen one's faith. This penetration will take place when we are conscious that they are words which are charged with tremendous potency. Having read them in the morning with this spirit, we can then commune with Bahá'u'lláh during the day at our work or wherever we may be and meditate on His words, so that like food which is absorbed into the body, these words may be absorbed into our hearts and souls. It is then that we will hunger to read more of the words in the evening. If we do not, it is a sign that we have not allowed the words to penetrate into our heart.

The Second Step

Allied with reading the writings, and comparable to it in the influence it can exert upon the soul, is Bahá'u'lláh's commandment of daily obligatory prayer. The obligatory prayer is different from other prayers in that it constitutes one of the major ordinances of Bahá'u'lláh and there are certain rites associated with it, including turning towards the Qiblih when reciting it in the privacy of one's own chamber. There are three obligatory prayers and the individual may choose any of the three.

Bahá'u'lláh has attached the utmost importance to this particular commandment. 'Abdu'l-Bahá in one of His Tablets describes the obligatory prayer as 'the very foundation of the Cause of God'[67] and the cause of spiritual life for the individual. In another Tablet He states that the observance of the ordinance of obligatory prayer is binding on all and no excuse is acceptable, except when a person is mentally deranged or is confronted by extraordinary circumstances.

It is impossible to draw nigh to Bahá'u'lláh without the daily observance of this important commandment.

Apart from obligatory prayers, which are enjoined on all believers, there are many prayers revealed by the Báb, Bahá'u'lláh and 'Abdu'l-Bahá which are of a different nature and the recital of which does not constitute a religious rite. Their recital is voluntary and can be done whenever the individual is moved to do so, either in private or public.

The Power of Prayer

Prayer, to become empty of self, is a vital necessity for spiritual growth. Our natural link with God is through prayer. A prayer which is without desire can exert a potent influence upon the soul. Through it the channels of God's grace will be opened and the outpouring of His bounties will refresh and invigorate the soul. Like a tree which, if alive, stretches its branches and leaves towards the sun to absorb its life-giving rays, the soul, if illumined with the light of faith, yearns for God in prayer, loves to extol Him and longs to commune with Him. If not, prayer may become an act of lip-service, devoid of joy and sincerity, and one's heart will then be unable to receive the outpouring of God's favours. A tree insensitive to the life-giving rays of the sun is dead, though the sun pours out its energies without ceasing. In the same way, the vivifying energies of God's infinite love are diffused throughout the whole of creation; yet not until we turn our hearts towards God in adoration can we become the recipient of these energies.

The power that can be generated in the heart of the believer, when freed from all desire and turned to God with songs of praise and glorification, is beyond our comprehension. Suffice it to say that many heroes of our Faith have derived their courage and steadfastness from this source. They used the power of prayer to teach and, as a result, became worthy instruments to bring thousands under the shadow of the Faith of Bahá'u'lláh.

The Third Step

Reading the words of Bahá'u'lláh, vital as this is, may not be conducive to spiritual progress unless it is combined with service to the Cause. Should a person take food regularly and in abundance but fail to move about and use one's muscles every day, one would soon become an invalid. In the same way, the reading of the writings must be accompanied by action. The greatest services to the Cause in this day are to teach the Faith as a daily obligation, to create Bahá'í communities and to raise up and consolidate Local Spiritual Assemblies everywhere.

Teaching, which is the act of conveying the message of God to a soul, has been given a pre-eminent position in this Dispensation. Not only has Bahá'u'lláh enjoined upon every believer the duty of teaching His Cause but He has regarded it as 'the most meritorious of all deeds'.[68] And 'Abdu'l-Bahá has stated, 'Of all the gifts of God the greatest is the gift of Teaching. It draweth unto us the Grace of God and is our first obligation.'[69]

The Fourth Step

The spiritual growth of the believer is also dependent upon pure and goodly deeds and obedience to the laws and teachings of Bahá'u'lláh. To live the life in accordance with the teachings of God is the goal of every Bahá'í. It is also a prerequisite of successful and effective teaching.

Bahá'u'lláh in one of His Tablets states:

> God hath prescribed unto every one the duty of teaching His Cause. Whoever ariseth to discharge this duty, must needs, ere he proclaimeth His Message, adorn himself with the ornament of an upright and praiseworthy character, so that his words may attract the hearts of such as are receptive to his call. Without it, he can never hope to influence his hearers.[70]

This statement leaves no room for doubt, for Bahá'u'lláh says, 'Without it, he can never hope to influence his hearers.' The word 'never' is very emphatic and rules out any other method. In numerous other Tablets Bahá'u'lláh has revealed similar statements.

The Protection of One's Faith

We observe in nature that when a child is born a most vital task then begins: the rearing of the child and its protection calls for loving care and vigilance on the part of its parents. It is the same with the spirit of faith. Once a person says 'I am a Bahá'í', that person must protect this most precious gift of faith and enable it to grow steadily.

The reading of the holy writings and the steps mentioned in these pages will put us on the highway of spiritual progress and bring us closer to Bahá'u'lláh.

The Three Great Robbers of Faith and Spirituality

As we tread this path of spiritual progress we need to be vigilant lest we are robbed of our faith by the forces of negation and ungodliness.

1) The first of these robbers is attachment to this world. The Bahá'í understanding of detachment is not that one must renounce the world and its affairs. Rather, anything that becomes a barrier between the believer and Bahá'u'lláh is attachment to this world. Love of oneself is the most formidable barrier. The greatest enemy that man has is the passion of his own self and ego.

2) The second robber of one's faith is bad company. Friendship with the ungodly may endanger or destroy one's faith. This is Bahá'u'lláh's ominous warning:

> O Son of Dust! Beware! Walk not with the ungodly and seek not fellowship with him, for such companionship turneth the radiance of the heart into infernal fire.[71]

The word 'ungodly' should not be misunderstood. An ungodly person may profess belief in God, while many who regard themselves as agnostics or atheists may not be ungodly in reality.

In contrast to this, we receive spiritual upliftment when we come into contact with someone who is on fire with the love of Bahá'u'lláh. The very company of such a person increases one's faith in God. Bahá'u'lláh states in the Hidden Words:

> He that seeketh to commune with God, let him betake himself to the companionship of His loved ones; and he that desireth to hearken unto the word of God, let him give ear to the words of His chosen ones.[72]

3) The third enemy is gossip and backbiting. To find fault in others and speak of it will undermine the very foundation of our faith in Bahá'u'lláh. He counsels us in these words:

> O Emigrants! The tongue I have designed for the mention of Me, defile it not with detraction. If the fire of self overcome you, remember your own faults and not the faults of My creatures, inasmuch as every one of you knoweth his own self better than he knoweth others.[73]

BIBLIOGRAPHY

'Abdu'l-Bahá. *The Promulgation of Universal Peace.* Wilmette, IL: Bahá'í Publishing Trust, 1982.

— *Selections from the Writings of 'Abdu'l-Bahá.* Haifa: Bahá'í World Centre, 1978.

— *The Will and Testament of 'Abdu'l-Bahá.* Wilmette, IL: Bahá'í Publishing Trust, 1971.

The Báb. *Selections from the Writings of the Báb.* Haifa: Bahá'í World Centre, 1976.

Bahá'í Journal (National Spiritual Assembly of the British Isles), August 1963.

Bahá'í Prayers: A Selection of Prayers revealed by Bahá'u'lláh, the Báb and 'Abdu'l-Bahá. Wilmette, IL: Bahá'í Publishing Trust, 2002.

Bahá'u'lláh. *Gleanings from the Writings of Bahá'u'lláh.* Wilmette, IL: Bahá'í Publishing Trust, 1983.

— *The Hidden Words.* Wilmette, IL: Bahá'í Publishing Trust, 1990.

— *The Kitáb-i-Aqdas.* Haifa: Bahá'í World Centre, 1992.

— *Kitáb-i-Íqán.* Wilmette, IL: Bahá'í Publishing Trust, 1989.

— *Tablets of Bahá'u'lláh revealed after the Kitáb-i-Aqdas.* Haifa: Bahá'í World Centre, 1978.

Britannica Book of the Year 2002. Chicago: Encyclopedia Britannica, 2002.

The Importance of Obligatory Prayer and Fasting. Oakham: Bahá'í Publishing, 2000.

Lights of Guidance: A Bahá'í Reference File. Compiled by Helen Hornby. New Delhi: Bahá'í Publishing Trust, 5th ed. 1997.

Nabíl-i-A'ẓam. *The Dawn-Breakers: Nabíl's Narrative of the Early Days of the Bahá'í Revelation.* Wilmette, IL: Bahá'í Publishing Trust, 1970.

Principles of Bahá'í Administration. London: Bahá'í Publishing Trust, 1976.

Shoghi Effendi. *Bahá'í Administration.* Wilmette, IL: Bahá'í Publishing Trust, 1968.

— *Dawn of a New Day: Messages to India 1923–1957.* New Delhi: Bahá'í Publishing Trust, 1970.

— *God Passes By.* Wilmette, IL: Bahá'í Publishing Trust, rev. ed. 1995.

— *Messages to America.* Wilmette, IL: Bahá'í Publishing Committee, 1947.

— *Messages to the Bahá'í World.* Wilmette, IL: Bahá'í Publishing Trust, 1971.

— *The World Order of Bahá'u'lláh.* Wilmette, IL: Bahá'í Publishing Trust, 1991.

The Universal House of Justice. Letter of the Universal House of Justice announcing the One Year Plan, 26 November 1999.

— Letter of the Universal House of Justice, Riḍván 2000.

— Letter of the Universal House of Justice to the World's Religious Leaders, April 2002.

— Letter of the Universal House of Justice, November 2007.

— *Messages from the Universal House of Justice 1963–1986: The Third Epoch of the Formative Age.* Wilmette, IL: Bahá'í Publishing Trust, 1996.

— *A Wider Horizon: Selected Messages of the Universal House of Justice 1983–1992.* Riviera Beach, FL: Palabra Publications, 1992.

NOTES AND REFERENCES

1. The Báb, *Selections*, p. 12.
2. Bahá'u'lláh, *Gleanings*, p. 11.
3. Bahá'u'lláh, quoted in Shoghi Effendi, *World Order*, pp. 106–7.
4. Bahá'u'lláh, *Gleanings*, pp. 92–3.
5. Bahá'u'lláh, quoted in Shoghi Effendi, *World Order*, p. 134.
6. Bahá'u'lláh, *Tablets*, p. 227.
7. 'Abdu'l-Bahá, *Will and Testament*, p. 3.
8. Mullá Ḥusayn, quoted in Nabíl, *Dawn-Breakers*, p. 341.
9. Bahá'u'lláh, *Gleanings*, p. 11.
10. 'Abdu'l-Bahá, *Will and Testament*, p. 3.
11. Shoghi Effendi, *God Passes By*, p. 324.
12. 'Abdu'l-Bahá, *Selections*, p. 88.
13. 'Abdu'l-Bahá, in *Bahá'í Prayers*, p. 333.
14. 'Abdu'l-Bahá, *Selections*, p. 87.
15. ibid. pp. 87–8.
16. ibid.
17. Bahá'u'lláh, *Kitáb-i-Aqdas*, para. 30.
18. Shoghi Effendi, *Bahá'í Administration*, p. 65.
19. 'Abdu'l-Bahá, *Selections*, p. 89.
20. 'Abdu'l-Bahá, *Promulgation*, pp. 72–3.
21. Shoghi Effendi, *Bahá'í Administration*, p. 88.
22. Shoghi Effendi, in *Principles of Bahá'í Administration*, p. 76.
23. ibid. pp. 44–5.
24. Bahá'u'lláh, *Gleanings*, p. 276.
25. A man who renounces the world in search of God and subsists on the charity of his fellow men.
26. 'Abdu'l-Bahá, *Selections*, p. 87.
27. From a letter written on behalf of Shoghi Effendi to an individual, 18 March 1950, quoted in *Bahá'í Journal*, August 1963.
28. 'Abdu'l-Bahá, *Selections*, p. 88.
29. ibid. p. 87.

30. Bahá'u'lláh, *Kitáb-i-Aqdas*, para. 30.
31. Shoghi Effendi, in *Lights of Guidance*, p. 487.
32. Shoghi Effendi, *God Passes By*, p. 214.
33. Shoghi Effendi, *Dawn of a New Day*, p. 176.
34. Shoghi Effendi, *Messages to the Bahá'í World*, p. 60.
35. ibid. p. 127.
36. ibid. p. 169.
37. ibid. p. 63.
38. Bahá'u'lláh, *Gleanings*, p. 170.
39. 'Abdu'l-Bahá, *Will and Testament*, p. 14.
40. Shoghi Effendi, in *Principles of Bahá'í Administration*, p. 77.
41. Shoghi Effendi, *World Order*, p. 7.
42. ibid. p. 89.
43. 'Abdu'l-Bahá, *Will and Testament*, pp. 19–20.
44. ibid. p. 20.
45. Universal House of Justice, *Messages 1963–1986*, p. 246.
46. Shoghi Effendi, *Messages to the Bahá'í World*, p. 155.
47. These figures at the time of printing in 2008 are markedly out of date. There has been an enormous expansion of the Faith throughout the world since the first publication of this book. The *Encyclopedia Britannica*, in its 2002 *Britannica Book of the Year*, indicated that the Bahá'í Faith was the second most widely spread religion in the world after Christianity.
48. Bahá'u'lláh, *Gleanings*, p. 7.
49. Bahá'u'lláh, Tablet of Aḥmad, in *Bahá'í Prayers*, p. 310.
50. Bahá'u'lláh, *Gleanings*, pp. 118–19.
51. Shoghi Effendi, *World Order*, pp. 156–7.
52. Letter of the Universal House of Justice announcing the One Year Plan, 26 November 1999.
53. Shoghi Effendi, *Messages to America*, p. 51.
54. Letter of the Universal House of Justice, Riḍván 2000.
55. Letter of the Universal House of Justice to the Bahá'ís of the World, 31 August 1987, in *Wider Horizon*, p. 53.
56. Letter of the Universal House of Justice, Riḍván 1996.
57. Letter of the Universal House of Justice, November 2007.
58. Letter of the Universal House of Justice to the World's Religious Leaders, April 2002.

59. Bahá'u'lláh, *Gleanings*, p. 70.
60. Ḥadíth, quoted in Bahá'u'lláh, *Kitáb-i-Íqán*, p. 46.
61. Bahá'u'lláh, *Hidden Words*, Arabic no. 59.
62. ibid. Persian no. 27.
63. ibid. Persian no. 26.
64. ibid. Arabic no. 42.
65. ibid. Persian no. 11.
66. Bahá'u'lláh, in *Bahá'í Prayers*, p. 4.
67. 'Abdu'l-Bahá, in *Importance of Obligatory Prayer and Fasting*, no. 35.
68. Bahá'u'lláh, *Gleanings*, p. 278.
69. 'Abdu'l-Bahá, *Will and Testament*, p. 25.
70. Bahá'u'lláh, *Gleanings*, p. 335.
71. Bahá'u'lláh, *Hidden Words*, Persian no. 57.
72. ibid. Persian no. 56.
73. ibid. Persian no. 66.

www.ingramcontent.com/pod-product-compliance
Ingram Content Group UK Ltd.
Pitfield, Milton Keynes, MK11 3LW, UK
UKHW020135250726
13967UKWH00002B/668

9 780853 985921